Advance Praise for Be~~thlehem~~ MW01026772

"Daniel Palmer preached from the Old Testament in Southeastern Seminary chapel over a decade ago, and I thank God often that I was in attendance that day. Daniel's handling of the text changed my life, because it pushed me to see Jesus on every page of Scripture. In this new book, Palmer walks readers through how to read the whole Bible as a book about Jesus and then shows us what reading with 'Christ-centered lenses' looks like from the book of Ruth. *Bethlehem's Redeemer* will not only push you to read Scripture in a way that's centered on Jesus, it will also push you toward Jesus through its pastoral and accessible tone. I highly recommend this gem of a book!"

Dr. Matthew Y. Emerson
Professor of Religion
Director, MACS and MAIS Programs
Dean, Hobbs College of Theology and Ministry

"Jesus is the hero of the whole Bible. There is no book that does not point in some way to His person and work. *Bethlehem's Redeemer* reveals His presence in each of the four chapters of the marvelous little book of Ruth. He is the true kinsman redeemer we all need."

Daniel L. Akin
President
Professor of Preaching & Theology
Southeastern Baptist Theological Seminary

"Rich enough to help pastors prepare to preach through the book of Ruth and accessible enough to help new believers better understand it, this book is a great devotional and study-help for anyone who wants to engage with these rich, beautiful stories of the Hebrew Scriptures more fully. Daniel makes even the cultural and theological nuances of Ruth easy to understand and helps the reader clearly see how to apply its principles."

J.D. Greear, Ph.D.
Pastor, The Summit Church, Raleigh-Durham, NC
62nd President, Southern Baptist Convention
Author, *What Are You Going to Do with Your Life?*

"Jesus said of the Old Testament, 'These are the very Scriptures that testify of me' (John 5:39). Daniel Palmer demonstrates how the Book of Ruth testifies of Jesus. He explains clearly how this little, beautiful Old Testament book reveals Jesus as our Kinsman Redeemer. *Bethlehem's Redeemer* is an excellent resource for any pastor, Sunday school teacher or small group leader who is preaching or teaching the Book of Ruth."

Kenneth Keathley
Senior Professor of Theology
Southeastern Baptist Theological Seminary

"Daniel Palmer blesses the reader with the mind of a serious student of God's Word, the shepherd's heart of a pastor, and a desire to point people to Jesus. Based off the Old Testament book of Ruth, the love of God and His great redemptive plan jumps off the pages as we are gripped by this epic real life story of mercy everlasting and hope eternal. Our Redeemer Lives!"

Brian Autry
Executive Director
SBC of Virginia

BETHLEHEM'S REDEEMER

Seeing Jesus in Ruth

Daniel J. Palmer

College&Clayton Press

ATHENS, GEORGIA

College&Clayton
Press

Scripture quotations taken from the New American Standard Bible® (NASB).
Copyright © 1960, 1962, 1963, 1968, 1971, 1972, 1973, 1975, 1977, 1995 by The
Lockman Foundation. Used by permission. www.Lockman.org.

Bethlehem's Redeemer: Seeing Jesus in Ruth
Copyright © 2020 Daniel J. Palmer
Revised 2021.

College and Clayton Press website: https://collegeandclayton.com

Cover Design: Daniel Blake Hulsey

ISBN: 978-1-7341915-4-7

Printed in the United States of America

This book is dedicated to my bride, Stacie, who is the best wife a pastor could ever hope for: selfless, resilient, forgiving, and beautiful inside and out. Without her loving support in all seasons, this work of love and offering to Christ would not have been possible.

Table of Contents

PREFACE

I n some ways, this little book has been in development for a long
time. Growing up as a pastor's kid came with a lot of unspoken
(and spoken!) pressure to follow in my father's footsteps. However,
my mom and dad wisely refused to push me and left God's calling in
God's hands. Christ saved me when I was 7, and I began sensing
God's call to vocational ministry in a church setting in my mid-
teens. However, I did not surrender to God's call until I was 27. In
the summer of 2005, my wife, Stacie, and I listed and sold our house
in four days and moved to Wake Forest, NC where I began studies
at Southeastern Baptist Theological Seminary.

Before studying at the seminary, I had been blessed to serve as a
Sunday School teacher where I developed a keen interest in the
connections between the Old Testament and Jesus. When I arrived
at seminary, I was eager to explore these connections more deeply.
However, I soon discovered that much of the formal study of the
Old Testament (and the New Testament too), at least at the
introductory level, was dedicated to understanding historical and
cultural backgrounds, debates about authorship and historicity, and
the (re)construction of the original setting for the book and the
situation in life of the original recipients of the book.

While these subjects are interesting and important for helping us
have confidence that God's Word is accurate and reliable, I began to
doubt the importance or even the possibility of seeing and
worshiping Christ in the Old Testament (other than when the New
Testament specifically cited an OT passage as referring to Jesus).

I was confident that God authored His perfect Word, but I was beginning to think the Old Testament was more about the people of
Israel than the promised Son of God. Connections I had seen as a
teenager, connections I truly believed the Holy Spirit had helped me
to see, were unraveling in my mind and heart.

During that time, on any given day, you would find a question like
one of these listed below bouncing around in my brain.

- When we read of fruit-bearing trees in Eden and then see
  that Christians are called to bear the fruit of the Spirit and
  spread the seed of the gospel, are these just coincidental
  uses of similar language, or is there something more to be
  learned about Jesus and life in Jesus in the Old Testament?
- When Abel, whose offering is accepted by the Lord, is a
  shepherd killed by his brother, are we learning something
  about the one who would be called "the Good Shepherd
  who lays down His life for the sheep" (John 10:11)?
- Is there a connection between the miraculous birth of a
  promised son to older women in the Old Testament and
  the miraculous conception of Jesus in the womb of a young
  virgin?
- When Jacob leaves home to find a bride and meets Rachel
  and then miraculously rolls a stone away from a well to give
  water to flocks of sheep, do we see something about Christ
  who leaves heaven to take a bride for Himself when a large
  stone is miraculously moved from the tomb, and He
  emerges as living water for His sheep?

The reason these questions were so important was because I was preparing to preach God's Word to God's people. If I could only show

Jesus from the Old Testament in exactly the places where the New Testament makes an explicit connection by alluding to or quoting from an Old Testament passage, how would I study the Old Testament? Is the Old Testament first a book about something other than knowing the Son of God and having life in Him and only secondarily and intermittently about knowing Jesus? If the entire Bible is inspired by God, but only spots of it are about the Son, how will we know when we are reading of Christ and when we are not?

Of course, seminary did not leave me in a state of doubt and confusion. The classes kept coming, and I slowly began to put the pieces back together. During this process, God sent me to a class that opened with this thundering pronouncement, "The Bible is not a book about how to live; it is a book about God's Son and how to have life in Him." Throughout the class, we were encouraged to "ask questions of the text" and to consider that, if the Holy Spirit wrote it all, there are surely intentional connections that point to Jesus and our life in Him. During that class, connections I had made in my teen years came rushing back. The Bible began to feed me in a fresh and powerful way as I saw connections between the Old and New Testaments and within the Old Testament itself. I could see Jesus throughout the Old Testament. Even when I could not see Him at first, I soon discovered that if I kept reading, sure enough, Jesus was there!

I began incorporating what I learned in the classroom and what the Spirit was showing me in the study into my weekly teaching (I was a Bible study teacher at the time). I saw people come alive with a newfound passion for encountering and worshiping Christ through Bible study. People stopped going to the Bible as a self-help manual and began seeking Christ in the Scriptures and celebrating Him in their lives. I discovered there is an amazing correlation between the intensity of the quest for Jesus in the Bible and the intensity of people's desire to honor Jesus in their daily lives.

In December of 2015, I moved to Roanoke, VA to serve Christ as
the Lead Pastor of the flock called North Roanoke Baptist Church.
Our church has a tradition of doing several Christmas sermons in
the Christmas season. For my first few Christmases, we worked
through some key passages in Luke, the genealogy in Matthew 1,
and then, again, some key portions of Luke's gospel.

As December 2018 was looming on the calendar, I felt I needed a
break from preaching the birth of Jesus from the gospels, and I decided to take what felt like a big risk. That first Sunday in December,
I stood in the pulpit and said, "Please take your copy of God's Word
and join me in turning to the book of Ruth." Over the next four
weeks, we learned much about the Savior born in Bethlehem by considering His life as revealed in Ruth.

The feedback I received from the series was incredibly humbling and
gratifying. People who have been Christians for decades said the
Bible was "coming alive," that they "loved Christ now more than
ever," and they were delighting in reading the Old Testament. While
there is nothing special about my sermons, there is something special about God's people growing in the adoration of God's Son because they have learned to see Him more clearly in God's Word.

As a pastor, I have become convinced that there is a direct correlation between seeking the Son in the Word and seeking to honor the
Son with our lives. The Holy Spirit uses the former to produce the
latter which means seeking Jesus in the stories of the Old Testament
is far more than a novel exercise; it is life for every follower of Christ
the Son.

When I decided to leave the gospels and preach on the gift of Christmas from an Old Testament book, Ruth seemed to be an obvious choice. The book is mostly set in Bethlehem, and it features the birth of a son though whom God brings redemption to a family and even a Gentile woman who had previously been separated from God's people with no hope of having a permanent place among them. The underlying connections to the birth of Jesus were too obvious to miss and too important to not proclaim.

As often happens, as I began to study Ruth, the Spirit opened my eyes to see Jesus in ways I had not anticipated. As I turned the Spirit's illumination into Christ-focused proclamation of Ruth, God gave eyes to my congregation to see as I had seen. He likewise filled their hearts with joy, praise, and worship of God's Son. In that moment, I sensed that, perhaps, the method of study and sermon preparation and resulting sermons could be an encouragement and model for pastors who want to preach Jesus from the Old Testament.

My hope is that this work will be a blessing to pastors considering a sermon series in Ruth and a book for all Christians who desire to seek and encounter Christ in the Old Testament. Jesus is Bethlehem's Redeemer, and we have much to learn about Him from the book of Ruth!

INTRODUCTION

The book of Ruth opens with these words, "Now it came about in the days when the judges governed, that there was a famine in the land" (1:1a).[1] The period of the judges was marked largely by a neglect of God's Word and, with some notable exceptions, judges who lost sight of the privilege of serving God and leading His people. The book of Judges concludes with these sobering words, "In those days there was no king in Israel; everyone did what was right in his own eyes" (Judges 21:25).

The concluding thought in Judges is that God's people need a king who will guide them into God's truth—the king the Lord promised to provide through the house of Judah (Gen 49:8–12). The opening of Ruth does not sound like the beginning of a story that leads to the provision of God's forever-king, but we should not be surprised that it is.

When God works at the height of human hopelessness, it puts an end to human boasting. Ruth, a book that begins with a famine and a family who leaves God's people for food among the people of

---

1. Scripture quotations taken from the *New American Standard Bible* (NASB) unless otherwise noted.

1

Moab, becomes a book that forms a bridge between a spiritual low point in Israel and the birth of David, who would be "a man after God's own heart" (1 Sam 13:14) and anointed King over God's people.

The book of Ruth ends with a natural segue into the life of David in 1 Samuel. As John Sailhamer writes, "The genealogy at the conclusion of the book makes the final link between this story and the birth of David—as well as the Son of David, the Messiah."[2] The significance of this observation is difficult to overstate. While Ruth is, according to Mary J. Evans, "an account, largely based on dialogue, of the life and concerns of one small Israelite family,"[3] it is not only that. To approach Ruth as a story of one family and only study the historical and cultural dynamics is to miss out on the book's primary message about God's coming promised Son and King.

My concern is that Christians often miss out on seeing the Son of God in the Old Testament, whether it is here in Ruth or many other Old Testament narratives. You might say there is an ongoing interpretive famine preventing us from feasting upon Christ as revealed in the Old Testament.

Interpreting Old Testament passages Messianically can rely on characters and phrases in the Bible to be understood figurally. Stephen Fowl observes how this practice can be important for understanding the book of Ruth.

> One traditionally Christian way of reading Old Testament texts is to read them figurally, especially to read them as prefiguring Christ. I think there are

2. John H. Sailhamer, *The Books of the Bible*, (Grand Rapids: Zondervan, 1998), 25.

3. Mary J. Evans, *Judges and Ruth*, The Tyndale Old Testament Commentaries (Downers Grove, IL: Inter-Varsity Press, 2017), 239.

> ways of reading such figures in Ruth....This practice
> of figural reading is not common anymore in either
> the academy or the church. It is, nevertheless, a
> crucial practice for reading theologically.[4]

Fowl is right in his assessment. There is a lack of reading and under-standing of the Old Testament in a Son-centric way. Rather than seeing the Son in the book of Ruth, emphasis is placed on improving communities. Fowl reflects further on this common emphasis.

> When modern commentaries do offer theological
> reflection on Ruth, they tend to treat the story as a
> dramatic example of the sort of care and concern
> God wishes Israel to show to widows and aliens in
> their midst....Christians reading Ruth would then
> be encouraged to make their communities similar
> places of welcome for widows and aliens. There is
> nothing wrong with this. The world needs such
> communities now more than ever.[5]

While the world does need God-honoring communities who exhibit God's care for the marginalized in society, and while it is not inaccurate to highlight these themes, such an approach is incomplete and harmfully inadequate. Any approach to the Old Testament that sidelines Jesus or tacks Him on as an afterthought does not reflect God's intention for His Word or serve God's people well. It is by encountering and embracing the Son in texts like Ruth that the church is enabled to create welcoming communities for widows and aliens. The faithful pastor and teacher and student of God's Word will want to help Christians see and worship God's Son as revealed not only in the New Testament but in the whole of God's Word.

---

4. Laura A. Smit and Stephen E. Fowl, *Judges and Ruth*, in *The Brazos Theological Commentary on the Bible*, (Grand Rapids: Brazos, 2018), 211.

5. Smit and Fowl, 210.

Without seeing and embracing the Son, people are powerless to keep God's commands. If we cannot proclaim the Son and life in the Son from the text, then what do we really have to proclaim? Charles Spurgeon offers an answer when he writes the following:

> Be much in hearing concerning Jesus. Souls by hundreds come to faith in Jesus under a ministry which sets him forth clearly and constantly. Few remain unbelieving under a preacher whose great subject is Christ crucified. Hear no minister of any other sort. There are such. I have heard of one who found in his pulpit Bible a paper bearing this text, "Sir, we would see Jesus." Go to the place of worship to see Jesus; and if you cannot even hear the mention of his name, take yourself off to another place where he is more thought of, and is therefore more likely to be present. Be much in reading about the Lord Jesus. The books of Scripture are the lilies among which he feedeth. The Bible is the window through which we may look and see our Lord.[6]

The coming Son of God and God's unmerited gift of life in Him is the overarching theme and message of the Old Testament, and, as we will see, it is the story of Ruth. The church desperately needs to see Jesus as the subject of the Old Testament because, as Jesus says, "This is eternal life, that they may know You, the only true God, and Jesus Christ whom You have sent" (John 17:3). When the church consistently sees Jesus in the Old Testament:

- It increases her knowledge and understanding of Him and His work in the here and now.
- It enables her to better understand the New Testament.
- It strengthens her faith in Him.

---

6. C. H. Spurgeon, *Around the Wicket Gate*, (New York: American Tract Society, 1890), 59–60.

- It deepens her love and appreciation and worship of the living Lord Jesus Christ, God's Son.[7]

Before diving into a method for seeing Christ in Old Testament narratives and applying it to Ruth, it will be helpful to understand why Jesus is infrequently proclaimed as the primary subject of the Old Testament.

WHY IS JESUS SELDOM SEEN IN THE PROCLAMATION OF THE OLD TESTAMENT?

It has not always been the case that Jesus has been overlooked in the church's preaching and teaching of the Old Testament. In the early church, some interpretations were so fanciful that they became warnings to today's pastors about the dangers of going beyond the plain or literal sense of the text.

In seminaries and colleges committed to the inerrancy and infallibility of God's Word, pastors and aspiring pastors were encouraged, rightly, to not exceed the plain meaning of the Scripture when teaching and applying it to their hearers. However, what is meant by "the plain sense" of God's Word became, in many contexts, overly restrictive. The fear of wrongly allegorizing was so great that many pastors became wary of asking questions about the text or pursuing thematic connections within the book and throughout the Scriptures.

In short, what was described as a plain-sense reading of the Bible became so restrictive that aspiring pastors were discouraged from

---

7. I thank God for the recent proliferation of resources designed to help the church see and appreciate Jesus in the Old Testament. For adults, consider picking up *The Story of Redemption Study Bible (ESV)*. For children, consider picking up a copy of *The Jesus Storybook Bible* and *The Big Picture Story Bible*. College and Clayton's forthcoming *Regarding the Bible* series uses a similar theological hermeneutic.

reading the Bible well. Reading the Bible well includes a theological interpretation. To read any given book of the Bible theologically means to read it as its author "intended it to be read." They had theological aims and included all the ingredients for a theological reading. Regarding such a theological reading of Matthew, scholar Charles Quarles maintains, "Matthew has packed his Gospel with all the cues and prompts necessary to read his gospel properly."[8] A similar statement could be made for every book in the Bible and for the Bible in its entirety. Learning to read the Bible in this way is an incredibly eye-opening and humbling experience. In his concluding paragraph, Quarles captures this well when he writes:

> Though I was raised in churches that had a strong commitment to the Bible, I must honestly confess that I did not learn to really read the Bible until I attended seminary. Before seminary, I read the Bible devotionally. To me that meant associating myself with one of the characters in the story. My false assumption, which now seems shockingly arrogant, was that the story was largely about me. I am now convinced that the Bible is to be read theologically as a book primarily about God, not me. I have discovered that a theological reading of Scripture is not less but more 'devotional' than my old approach. As I discover God's glory and majesty revealed on page after page of the Bible, I am compelled to worship Him and devote myself to Him like never before.[9]

Seminary had a similar impact in my life. In recent years, increasing numbers of professors are encouraging this approach. Pastors who prepare at top-rate seminaries are still required, as they were years ago, to learn the biblical languages and rightly divide God's Word,

---

8. Charles Quarles, "How to Read Matthew Theologically," *Credo Magazine* (December 30, 2019). Accessed from https://credomag.com/2019/12/how-to-read-matthew-theologically/.

9. Quarles, 2019.

but there is a greater emphasis on reading theologically and with an appreciation that God's Son is the subject of the entire Bible.[10] My father and I attended seminaries sponsored by the same denomination, but the dates on our degrees are separated by 31 years. While my father and I had very similar courses in Biblical exposition, he largely missed out on the benefits having professors who emphasized the importance of reading theologically (and I would add Christo-centrically). Today, I often hear him say, "I wish someone had shared this with me in seminary." As he has discovered, a plain-sense reading of the Bible supports a theological reading of the Scriptures. A theological reading of the Bible, seeing that the Bible is about God's Son, is not something superimposed upon the text but something derived from a careful study of the Scriptures. The Bible is God's revelation of Himself to us, and an accurate plain-sense reading of the text will support the conclusion that the stories and the story of the Old Testament are about God's Son.

While some have missed out on the joy of seeing and considering Jesus in the Old Testament because of a fear of misusing the text, other pastors simply do not have the time to try. Seeing Jesus in the Old Testament takes time for study, prayer, and meditation. It takes reading the Scriptures in their entirety—not just once, but regularly.

PASTORS AND PREACHING ACCORDING TO THE SCRIPTURES

It is too often the case that pastors are unable to spend the time necessary to confidently exalt Christ from the Old Testament because

---

10. Sadly, some seminaries have trimmed the overall hours required for a Master of Divinity and reduced or eliminated the Biblical-language requirements. Making theological connections within a book of the Bible (intratextuality) and across the Scriptures (intertextuality) is important, but it is also important that the connections genuinely exist, and being able to compare and analyze words in the original language is an important part of that process.

they are taking care of the "other duties" that often come with leadership, management, programming, counseling, funerals, budgets, meetings, conflict, etc. If you are a layperson, one of the best things you can do for your church's spiritual growth and development is appreciate and encourage your pastor's time in his study.

While some pastors are pressed for time and their study suffers, others are not too different from the ungodly leaders in the book of Judges. When they "preach" the Old Testament, they appeal to "itching ears" (2 Tim 4:3) rather than preach Christ crucified.

It is not unusual for pastors to select verses out of context and piece them together into a "sermon" that has more in common with the New Age movement, manifestation boards, and the power of positive thinking than with the "faith once and for all delivered to the saints" (Jude 3). Passages about wealth and blessing are among the most routinely-exploited verses. In these sermons, Jesus, if He is mentioned at all, sounds more like a genie in a bottle than the Maker of Heaven and earth to Whom every knee must bow.

Whether it is a personality preacher or a prosperity preacher, what is missing from many sermons is a clear and sustained focus on the Person and work of Jesus Christ. Personality and prosperity sermons do not magnify Christ as the hero and rescuer of God's people.

If you are a layperson in a church with a pastor who preaches through books of the Bible and aspires to exalt Jesus, thank and encourage him to continue "in season and out of season" (2 Tim 4:2). If you are a pastor, keep resisting the pressure to perform and to please. Never trade "being relevant" for faithfully proclaiming what God has revealed about His Son and the life that is available in Him and in Him alone. Christ is always relevant. When your preaching ministry is over, to the extent that you have proclaimed Christ according to the Scriptures, your preaching will endure.

While some pastors are too pressed for time and some twist the Scriptures to tickle itching ears or promote themselves, many pastors and Christians want to engage the Old Testament more frequently and in a Christ-focused way, but they are too overwhelmed to begin.

For a variety of reasons, the Old Testament often seems daunting to pastors, teachers, and everyday believers alike. As noted above, some pastors were discouraged in their theological training from "going overboard" in seeing Jesus in the Old Testament, and now some fear seeing Him there at all. The fear that came from the academy moved to the pulpit, and as a result, laypeople are likewise often fearful of engaging with the Old Testament. This is not as it should be. The Scriptures of the first believers were the Old Testament, and Jesus is who the Old Testament reveals Him to be. Seeing Jesus in the Old Testament is a matter of better knowing our King.

But, if this is the case, if the Old Testament points to and anticipates the coming of God's Son, pastors and churches need to be encouraged to see Him there. This book is for pastors, worship leaders, Bible-study teachers, and everyday Christians who want to see Jesus in the Old Testament. Before we get to the example of Ruth, it is important to remember why we should expect to see Jesus in the Old Testament.

ATTEMPTS TO UNDERMINE THE WITNESS OF THE OLD TESTAMENT

While it should go without saying that we should expect to read God's message about His Son within the pages of the Old Testament, it unfortunately cannot. For various reasons, the meaning, purpose, and even the existence of a recognized and authoritative Old Testament has been debated and questioned for as long as the church has been in existence.

As we endeavor to see the Son in the Old Testament, we must understand that we can have confidence in the Old Testament. The Old Testament that we regard as Scripture today is the Old Testament that has been recognized as authoritative, accurate, and divinely-authored Scripture throughout the history of the church (and before the coming of Christ by the people of God). The canon did not appear out of thin air, and the church did not "create" the canon; the people of God recognized the canon.

The purpose of producing a recognized list of the authoritative works of Scripture was not primarily to settle doubts within the Church about what is and what is not divinely-inspired Scripture. To be sure, there were a few books debated along the way; however, the church demonstrates widespread agreement on the books included in the Old Testament and the divine authority of the Old Testament.

The canon assisted the Church in recognizing false teachers and false teachings, and false teaching has been abundant from the day of Christ's ascension to this day. The ongoing threat of false teaching forced the leaders of the early churches to defend their faith in the crucified, resurrected, and reigning Christ, and they did so from what they recognized as Scripture. By God's grace, enough of their writings were preserved such that we can know beyond any reasonable doubt that the true people of God have always professed and proclaimed a faith in Christ as revealed in what we know as the Bible—Old and New Testaments.

A shining example of the defense of the Old Testament as a book about Jesus comes in Irenaeus's *Adversus Haereses* or *Against Heresies*.[11] Approximately 125 years after Christ's ascension, he writes to counter Gnostics who invented an entirely different version of the origins of the world and superimposed it upon their reading of the Old Testament. Irenaeus counters the warped worldview of the Gnostics, going verse-by-verse through their arguments. He recognizes the "writings of the evangelist and the apostles" and "the law and the prophets" as Scripture.[12] Later, he affirms the four Gospels—no more and no less—are Scripture.[13] While some, to this day, wrongly suggest the church was uncertain about what qualified as Scripture for centuries after the coming of Christ, the evidence proves otherwise. The writings of Irenaeus demonstrate the existence of a functional canon much earlier in the life of the Church including a clear refutation of "apocryphal and spurious writings" such as the Gospel of Thomas.[14]

Irenaeus is by no means the only Christian writer who helps us see the church is founded by and upon Christ as revealed in a well-defined and authoritative Old Testament. In addition to the many extant writings from the early church Fathers demonstrating the existence of an early functional canon, we also have evidence from those who were opposed to the church and to the God revealed in the Bible. As Andreas Köstenberger, Scott Kellum, and Charles Quarles write, "Around 140, the heretic Marcion in Rome declared an edited Gospel of Luke and only 10 letters of Paul as useful while rejecting all the other apostolic works, which necessitated a response

---

11. Irenaeus (c. 125–202) was a bishop who learned from Bishop Polycarp who in turn had learned from the Apostle John.

12. Irenaeus, *Against Heresies*, 1.3.6. Read a translation of this work at the Christian Classics Ethereal Library (https://ccel.org/).

13. Irenaeus, 3.11.8.

14. Irenaeus, 1.10.1.

by those in the apostolic mainstream of Christianity."[15] Marcion
saw in the Old Testament a different god than the God who forgives
in the New, so he rejected the Old Testament all-together and cre-
ated his own edited version of the New Testament, a version elim-
inating Old Testament references. Marcion's awareness of which
books and references to eliminate to justify his conception of god
likewise demonstrates there was a widespread acceptance of what we
regard as the Old Testament for him to refute just 100 years or so
after the resurrection of Jesus. From her earliest days, the true
church of God has known what the Old Testament is, and she has
confessed that it is a book about Jesus, the Son of God.

So, for centuries, the church has been confronted with twin challenges:

- some, disregarding clear evidence to the contrary, reject the
  existence of a settled and authoritative word from God, and
- others agree the Old Testament has an authority, but they
  do not read it as revelation about God's Son and having life
  in Him.

In his battle with the Gnostics, Irenaeus was refuting heretics who
claimed to read the Old Testament literally, but the Gnostics
brought to the Bible an interpretive grid that necessarily came from
outside of it. They did not view the Scriptures as closed but merely
one source among others for experiencing truth in the heart. As a
result, Irenaeus did more than examine the particulars of any given
passage, he argued that the Bible supplies its own interpretive rule,
the rule of faith or the rule of truth. As John Behr summarizes it,
"God's work in Christ...gives the form and direction to this exege-

---

15. Andreas J. Köstenberger, L. Scott Kellum, and Charles L. Quarles,
The Lion and the Lamb, (Nashville: B&H Publishing, 2012), 5–6.

sis."[16] In other words, the people of God down through the generations have not merely been a people who lived by faith but by faith in the Son of God, a Son revealed to them in the Scriptures rightly divided and rightly understood. To understand the Old Testament, it must be read as a witness to the Son of God.

Ultimately, the Church recognized the works of Scripture by seeing within them a consistent witness to the Son of God. Furthermore, the Church recognized and refuted false teaching by insisting the Scriptures be read as a witness to the Son of God. Unfortunately, to this day, some theological systems suggest the Old Testament, especially the Mosaic code, only applies to the Jews, and largely dismiss the relevance of much of the Old Testament for knowing Christ. As we will see momentarily, Jesus and the apostles had a very different way of reading the Old Testament.

For them, and for the people of God in every generation, our hope is found in the Son of God who is promised in Genesis 3:15 and revealed throughout the Old Testament. The Old Testament is not a book for a bygone era; it is God's living and active Word about our great need and God's great provision in His Son. The Old Testament is a reliable witness to the Son of God, painting a picture for us of who the Messiah would be and urging us to seek and honor God's Son.

WHY SHOULD WE EXPECT TO SEE JESUS IN THE OLD TESTAMENT?

As noted in the previous section, some theologians largely write off the Old Testament as pertaining only or primarily to ethnic Jews. This reading of the Old Testament differs markedly from that of

---

16. John Behr, "Scripture, the Gospel, and Orthodoxy," *St. Vladimir's Theological Quarterly* 43, no. 3 (1999): 225.

Jesus and His apostles. For them, and for the early church, the Old Testament was not "Jewish Scripture" but Scripture—God's revelation of Himself to all people. In John 5:39–47, Jesus charges the Pharisees with reading the Old Testament wrongly. They were looking for rules and saying they believed Moses, but Jesus tells them, essentially, "Moses was not writing about rules; He was writing about Me."

The Apostle Paul also laments that many of his Jewish brothers read the Old Testament as Scripture about Judaism rather than Scripture about Messiah because, "...their minds were hardened; for until this very day at the reading of the old covenant the same veil remains unlifted, because it is removed in Christ. But to this day whenever Moses is read, a veil lies over their heart" (2 Cor 3:14–15). Christians have the great joy of reading, interpreting, and understanding the Old Testament with unveiled hearts—with Spirit-given eyes to behold the Son of God. As we will see, the apostles read the Old Testament as a direct, not a distant or derivative, witness to Jesus and life in Him. Before considering the perspective of the apostles, we will consider how Jesus described the witness of the Old Testament.

Jesus' Perspective on Himself as the Subject of the Old Testament

As Christ rescues sinners, He gives them eyes to see Him in the Old Testament. We know the Old Testament was recognized as Scripture in the days of Jesus because Jesus spoke of the recognized Hebrew divisions of the Old Testament—the Law, Prophets, and Writings (in Luke 24:44, Jesus uses "the Law of Moses and the Prophets and the Psalms")—as authoritative Scripture. In Luke 4, when Jesus is preaching at the synagogue in his hometown of Nazareth, we read,

> And the book of the prophet Isaiah was handed to
> Him. And He opened the book and found the place

> where it was written, "The Spirit of the Lord is upon Me, because He anointed Me to preach the gospel to the poor. He has sent Me to proclaim release to the captives, and recovery of sight to the blind, to set free those who are oppressed, to proclaim the favorable year of the Lord." And He closed the book, gave it back to the attendant and sat down; and the eyes of all in the synagogue were fixed on Him. And He began to say to them, "Today this Scripture has been fulfilled in your hearing" (Luke 4:17–21).

Jesus says that Isaiah speaks of Him. But Jesus goes much further than quoting from a lone passage in Isaiah in establishing that He is the subject of the Old Testament. His argument is not that a mere proof-texted version of the Old Testament speaks of Him, but that the entire Old Testament testifies of Jesus.

In Luke 24, when two disciples walked with Jesus on the road to Emmaus, we read that,

> He said to them, "O foolish men and slow of heart to believe in *all* that the prophets have spoken! Was it not necessary for the Christ to suffer these things and to enter into His glory?" Then beginning with Moses and with *all* the prophets, He explained to them the things concerning Himself in *all* the Scriptures (Luke 24:25–27, emphasis mine).

Jesus explained the Old Testament to his disciples Christologically and then broke bread with them. Interestingly, Ruth uses the theme of grain or bread to point to God's miraculous provision through His Son, and it was not until the disciples ate bread with the Bread of Life that they recognized Him. As the person of God's provision is with them, their eyes are opened not only to see Jesus but to see Him as Christ according to the Scriptures.

Just a bit later, Jesus is with other disciples, and He declares not only that the Old Testament is about Him but that it is about the progress of the gospel among all the nations. As Luke records later in chapter 24,

> Now He [Jesus] said to them, "These are My words which I spoke to you while I was still with you, that all things which are written about Me in the Law of Moses and the Prophets and the Psalms must be fulfilled." Then He opened their minds to understand the Scriptures, and He said to them, "Thus it is written, that the Christ would suffer and rise again from the dead the third day, and that repentance for forgiveness of sins would be proclaimed in His name to all the nations, beginning from Jerusalem" (Luke 24:44–47).

According to Jesus, His death and resurrection and the proclamation of the gospel to all the nations is the subject of every genre of the Old Testament. All of this is in the Old Testament, and as we will see, much of it is in Ruth.

While Luke 4 and Luke 24 clearly demonstrate Jesus sees Himself as the subject of the Old Testament, Luke 16 offers a different twist on the same information. In the story of the rich man and Lazarus, both men die. While poor Lazarus is in Abraham's bosom, the rich man is in torment in Hades. The rich man asks Abraham to send Lazarus over with water to cool his tongue. This is not possible because of a great chasm between the place of paradise and the place of judgment and torment. Instead, the rich man asks Abraham to send Lazarus to warn his five living brothers about the coming judgment, but Abraham said,

> "They have Moses and the Prophets; let them hear them." But he [the rich man] said, "No, father Abraham, but if someone goes to them from the

> dead, they will repent!" But he [Abraham] said to
> him, "If they do not listen to Moses and the
> Prophets, they will not be persuaded even if
> someone rises from the dead" (Luke 16:29–31).

We should feel the weight and the bliss of this profound truth. Because God has chosen to reveal His Son by way of His Word, the witness of Moses and the Prophets rightly proclaimed is a more reliable witness to Jesus than a physical sighting of Him raised from the dead. When we stand to preach Christ according to the Old Testament, we participate in God's ordained way of revealing His Son and convincing sinners of their need for Him. As Paul says, "For the word of the cross is foolishness to those who are perishing, but to us who are being saved it is the power of God" (1 Cor 1:18). When our proclamation is consistent with the intended purpose of God's message, God works through the "foolishness" of preaching to help others behold and trust His Son.

The Apostles' Perspective on Jesus as the Subject of the Old Testament

After Jesus ascended to the right hand of the Father, His apostles shared His reading of the Old Testament. In his first recorded sermon, Peter quotes from Joel 2:28–32, Psalm 16:8–11, and Psalm 110:1 with the understanding that these texts speak of the death and resurrection of Jesus and the Spirit-empowered community who would follow Him. Of Psalm 16, Peter says that David, "looked ahead and spoke of the resurrection of the Christ" (Acts 2:31). Peter's sermon tells us in Acts that the writers of the Old Testament were not writing for themselves, but for those who would have confidence in Christ and salvation in Him because of what they wrote about Him.

As to this salvation, the prophets who prophesied of the grace that would come to you made careful searches and inquiries, seeking to know what person or time the Spirit of Christ within them was indicating as He predicted the sufferings of Christ and the glories to follow. It was revealed to them that they were not serving themselves, but you (Acts 2:10–12).

Later, in 2 Peter, after the apostle recalls hearing the voice of the Father from heaven saying "This is My beloved Son...," Peter says that, as impressive as that was, the Scriptures are a more reliable witness to who Jesus is. He writes, "So we have the even more sure prophetic word to which you do well to pay attention as to a lamp shining in a dark place, until the day dawns and the morning star arises in your hearts" (2 Pet 1:19). Peter is not the only Apostle to speak of the Old Testament as being about the Christ. Paul used this same interpretive strategy.

In Acts, we learn that when Paul arrived in a new city, he would spend three Sabbath days in the synagogue "explaining and giving evidence that the Christ had to suffer and rise again from the dead, and saying, 'This Jesus whom I am proclaiming to you is the Christ'" (Acts 17:3). Later, when Paul reminds us the gospel is of first importance, he says the gospel includes that Jesus died, was buried, and was raised "*according to the* [Old Testament] *Scriptures*" (1 Cor 15:3–4, emphasis mine). The gospel, according to Paul, must be understood and proclaimed as a gospel revealed in the Old Testament. Indeed, the operating assumption of the New Testament writers is that the Old Testament is about the Son of God and having life everlasting in and under His righteous reign. If the New Testament writers understood the Old Testament to be God's story about His Son, we must likewise read the Old Testament as the story of Christ and the life His followers live through Him.[17]

HOW TO SEE CHRIST IN THE OLD TESTAMENT

While it is clear Jesus is the subject of the Old Testament, it is perhaps not as clear how to go about seeing Jesus in the Old Testament and then to preach and teach in such a way that others may see Him as well. For people to see what we see, it is helpful for them to be taught how we developed our vision. In this section, I share my method for seeing the Son of God in the Old Testament narratives—a method developed from a combination of reading and study along with trial and error.

This is the method I used when preparing messages from Ruth. There is nothing special about my method other than that it works well for me, and it includes the foundational steps of reading, study, prayer, and meditation—steps which should be included in any system of preparing to preach and/or teach God's Word.

---

17. It is common to read about a "dual fulfillment" of the Old Testament. In this reading of the Old Testament, the fulfillment of the Old Testament is often conceived of as a mountain range in the distance with the nearer fulfillment being those mountains that are close on the horizon and the fulfillment in Christ being those mountains that are distant. While this is a prevailing view, it does not square well with the witness of the New Testament, which strongly suggests the Old Testament writers understood themselves to be writing of the distant reality of Christ's coming and not for themselves. This understanding renders a fulfillment other than the fulfillment in Christ unnecessary. Or, if there is a dual fulfillment, it is the fulfillment in Christ that is the primary fulfillment in the mind of the Spirit as He inspires the Scriptures. For this reason, and because the opening story in the Old Testament concludes with an implicit call to search for the Son of God who would reverse the curse of the Fall of Adam described in the Scriptures that follow, we stand on solid, biblical, and Christ-honoring ground in reading the Old Testament as a quest to know, see, understand, worship, and embrace the promised Son of God.

Step 1: Believe God has Given Us His Word to Reveal His Son

When reading the Old Testament, we must go with unwavering confidence that God has revealed His Son in the Old Testament, and He desires for us to encounter Jesus there. I am not suggesting that we have faith in faith but faith in God who has spoken. The Father desires to glorify the Son, the Spirit who inspired the Scripture has been sent to help us, and the goal of His help is that we would glorify the Son (John 16:14). When we come to the Old Testament to see and embrace life in the Son, we come with a proper motivation that pleases God. God honors our pursuit of His Son because it is consistent with the purpose for which He gave the message.

Step 2: Pray

When I begin a new study, I ask God to open my heart and mind to read with understanding. When I am in the Old Testament, I ask God to open my eyes to behold His Son. While I pray in a similar way before every new study, it is not a mere routine. When we pray, we come humbly and desperately. Earnest prayer is the medicine God uses to rid us of presumption or personal agendas that would otherwise cloud our view of God's Son. Unless the Spirit gives us the spiritual eyes to see what we need to see, and unless He impresses His vision of His Son upon us, all the best resources in the world will not help us. The door to delighting in God's Son as revealed in the Old Testament is genuine desperation to know and encounter Him in the text. We cannot know the risen, ascended, and reigning Son of God apart from knowing Him as revealed in the Bible. Before we read or study—and during our reading and studying—we must pray.

Step 3: Read a Short Summary of the Story

Although I am continually reading through the Scriptures, I still find that reading a little refresher on the overall flow and storyline of any book of the Bible before I begin preparing to preach it helps me considerably in my comprehension and study. Having a summary of the flow of the book helps me glean more from the story when I read it all the way through. I highly recommend Sailhamer's *The Books of the Bible* or the excellent introductory videos available from the Bible Project.[18]

Step 4: Read the Story All the Way Through

Pastors, teachers, and small group leaders are familiar with looming deadlines. Sunday and Wednesday nights are always coming. When one lesson is complete, the next one is due within days. One of the reasons God designed the local church with a plurality of pastors is so that each pastor would have the time to truly study. If you are the primary preaching pastor for your church, I strongly recommend asking other pastors on staff to give you a one or two week break from your preaching duties when transitioning from one series to the next. This will not be "time off" but time well spent in deep reading and study. Good sermons do not come from commentaries or websites; they come from a deep time of communing with God in the study.

When I sit down to begin a new series, the temptation that I face on every occasion is to go straight to the commentaries and the work of parsing and translating the original languages. These steps are important, but in my experience, they cannot come first. To see the Son in the text of Scripture, and particularly in the Old Testament,

---

18. Videos for each book of the Bible are available from https://bibleproject.com/. John Sailhamer's *The Books of the Bible* is referenced in footnote 2.

one must read the story all the way through and preferably several times. On my first reading, I just read. On my second reading, I note repeated themes and phrases. On my last reading, I make note of the major divisions of thought or movements of plot within the story and jot down ideas and questions for deeper exploration.

This work takes time, but it pays huge dividends in the work that follows. For example, if we were to pray, read, study, and prepare a sermon from Ruth 1 without reading the entire story at the outset, we may forget specifically how the story concludes in chapter 4. If we do not see the end of chapter 4, we will likely miss much of the significance of the book's introduction in chapter 1. The period of the judges was a mess because the people did not have a godly king, and the book ends with the assurance that God's people will have a king. In the midst of moral failure and famine, God has not stopped working, and the promise of a Son to rescue His people has not been abandoned. God mercifully provides to redeem a family and ultimately all of His people through an unlikely son born of the tribe of Judah in Bethlehem.

Step 5: Ask Questions of the Text

Some of the steps in this process of study and preparation are really more an ongoing practice throughout rather than a defined step. I find that I am constantly asking and refining key questions about the text. It is helpful to keep a running list of questions for examination when you translate the text, read the commentaries, and chase down other Scriptures that help answer your questions. After reading the text through, I recommend pausing to write down all the questions that come to mind. You can always refine, consolidate, and eliminate questions later. Of all the "steps" in this process, this has proven to be among the most helpful. The process of asking questions leads in several directions—across the entire story, deep into a verse or paragraph that needs greater explanation, and out to God's people as I consider how to encourage God's people to apply themselves to the life they have in the Son.

Following each chapter on the book of Ruth, I list some key questions I asked in the process of studying and writing each sermon in a section titled Questions for Pastors and Teachers. My hope is that seeing the sermon and the questions will help illustrate this part of the process of sermon/lesson preparation.

Step 6: Pay Special Attention to the Son of Promise

I will never forget the day I realized that at any given time in the Old Testament, out of all the people mentioned in the story, there is only one possible person who can fulfill the promises of God. I was reading Genesis, and I came to the beginning of chapter 22 dealing with the story of the testing of Abraham.

> Now it came about after these things, that God tested Abraham, and said to him, "Abraham!" And he said, "Here I am." He said, "Take now your son, your only son, whom you love, Isaac, and go to the land of Moriah, and offer him there as a burnt offering on one of the mountains of which I will tell you" (Gen 22:1–2).

I had read through Genesis many times, but I had never been struck by the words "your son, your only son" as I was that afternoon. Abraham had another son—Ishmael! In that moment, I was forced to reckon with this question, "In what sense is Isaac the only son of Abraham?" The answer is that Isaac, at that moment in the story, is the only son through whom God's promises to Abraham could be realized. Isaac is the only son of promise in the story. He is the main character God will use to reveal to us the eventual and ultimate Son of Promise. God had already said His blessings would not come through Ishmael. Abraham would eventually be the father of a great nation, a source of blessing to all the families living on the earth, and have a great name through God's promised Son (Gen 12:1–3). Without the one promised Son of God, the promises would not be realized. And, at that point in the story, Isaac is the only son in all the world who could possibly be the son that God would use to fulfill His promises. As the story continues, there remains only one possible son of promise until we arrive at the Son of Promise. Isaac and Rebekah have the twins Jacob and Esau, and before their births, God announces the promises must come through Jacob who is later given the name Israel. Before Israel is ever a nation comprised of many sons, she is a single son. This is a picture of the reality that the many who becomes sons and daughters of the Father must be made new in Jesus, the one Son of Promise. To belong to God as His sons and daughters, we must be adopted, born again, and made new in His Son.

God shows us in Genesis 22, while there are many sons, there is still only one son who really matters in terms of the fulfillment of the promises of God. We have good reason to look for "the only son" as we read through Old Testament stories. While these sons of promise are not "the Son of Promise," God is writing one story about His Son through their stories. Obviously, not every story in the Old Testament affords us this direct opportunity, but many, including Ruth, do. Indeed, the book of Ruth mentions several sons of promise: Perez "whom Tamar bore to Judah" (Ruth 4:12), along with Hezron, Ram, Amminadab, Nashon, Salmon, Boaz, Obed, Jesse, and David.

Because we have read the entire story, and because we have looked for the son of promise in the text, we realize upon reflection that the death of Naomi's sons (Ruth 1:5) ends up leading her back to Bethlehem where a family that was as good as dead is restored and given a standing in the land among God's people through the birth of another son. As Christmas was coming, and I decided to pursue the book of Ruth, I primarily had in mind the connection between the birth of a baby in Bethlehem in Ruth and Christ's birth in Bethlehem. What I soon discovered, because I was looking to learn what God was showing me about His Promised Son through the promised sons, is that God shows us much more in Ruth than I had at first suspected about Jesus, the Redeemer born in Bethlehem.

Step 7: Closely Evaluate the Text and Read the Commentaries

After reading the story through a few times noting key questions and paying attention to the son of promise, it is helpful to ensure that your assessment of repeated words, phrases, or themes genuinely exists in the text. Because the Bible was not originally written in English, there are times when variances in translation may lead us to conclude there is a thematic connection where none exits. Alternatively, there are times when an identical word in Hebrew or Greek is translated in multiple ways in our English translations, and we may miss a thematic connection that does exist in the text. If you do not have any familiarity with the original languages, that does not mean you cannot study the Bible. Excellent commentaries and study material are available that will identify and address many of these issues.[19]

After working through the text, I read through several commentaries comparing my insights and observations with those that

---

19. While I have studied the original languages, I am by no means an expert. For study in the Old Testament, I have found the series of commentaries titled A Handbook on the Hebrew Text to be exceptionally helpful. For Ruth, I often consulted Robert D. Holmstedt, *Ruth, A Handbook on the Hebrew Text* (Waco, TX: Baylor U Press, 2010).

others have made. Commentaries will often provide references to other portions of Scripture where similar themes are addressed. For example, as I explored the idea that God's Son is portrayed as a kinsman-redeemer in Ruth, I was directed to several passages from the writings of Moses that speak of God as redeemer and of laws related to the redemption of a widow left with no son to provide for her or carry on her family's name in the land. After getting to this point in your preparation, there is an understandable desire to begin writing, but another important step remains.

Step 8: Mediate (or Let it Settle)

Though it has been some time ago now, I can still hear a nightly conversation I had with my mom after supper in the summertime. The sun was still shining, and the neighborhood kids were playing, and I would ask to join them. Mom, almost invariably, would say, "Yes, once you let your food settle." She never made me wait too long, but she knew that I needed to wait a few moments because I only knew one speed as a youngster—wide open!

I am not physically as quick as I was in those days, but I still tend to want to rush to the next thing. It is possible to rush the process of preparing a sermon, Bible study, or Sunday School lesson. When you do not know what the week will hold in terms of funerals and other unexpected challenges, there is a always a pressure to press on and finish the sermon, but pressing too much too quickly prevents us from digesting all that we have feasted upon in God's Word.

The opposite of moving too quickly from reading and study to writing the sermon or lesson is meditation. Meditation is not emptying our minds but filling them with God's truth. As Martin Luther writes,

> Thus you see in this same Psalm (119) how David constantly boasts that he will talk, meditate, speak, sing, hear, read by day and night and always, about nothing except God's Word and commandments. For God will not give you his Spirit without the eternal Word; so take your cue from that.[20]

For Luther, Psalm 119 demonstrated that meditating on the Scriptures was a necessary step to be impacted by the Spirit as you study.

The Psalter includes multiple references to meditating on God's Word including in the very first Psalm where we read of the blessed man who meditates on the law of the Lord, "day and night" (Psalm 1:2). In my experience, the meditations after a day of reading, prayer, and study can wander all over the place. I recall reading through Ruth and wondering how I could ever do justice to all God was showing me in just four sermons. I suspect that is why God speaks of meditation that occurs "day and night." God often sorts out what He has shown me as I sleep. Sometimes, the Spirit will wake me up with thoughts and observations to write down and then pick up the next morning. When we go to sleep with God's Word in our minds and hearts, the Spirit works to give us understanding and fresh energy to turn our study into a sermon about God's Son and having life in Him. In the long run, sermon preparation is richer, more rewarding, and proceeds more efficiently after a season of intentional meditation on the Word of God.

APPLYING OURSELVES TO THE CHRIST WE SEE IN THE OLD TESTAMENT

We live in a "do-it-yourself, can-do, figure-it-out-on-YouTube" world, and that is a challenge when it comes to sermon preparation

---

20. Martin Luther, "Preface to the Wittenberg Edition of Luther's German Writings" in *Martin Luther's Basic Theological Writings* 2nd ed., edited by Timothy Lull (Minneapolis, Fortress Press, 2005), 72–73.

because the gospel begins not with our ability but our inability. The gospel is good news not because of what we can do or what we have done but because of what God does for us through His Son. If we seek the Son and life in Him in the Old Testament, we will soon learn that we must think less about applying the Scripture to our lives and more of applying our lives to the Scripture.

If there is only one son of promise in the text, and if all the promises of God must come through that son, we are not the son of promise. We are not the hero of the story. The story of David is not about how we can slay our giants. We cannot slay anything of spiritual significance that comes against us, but Christ our conquering King— of whom the unlikely and trusting David is a type—can.

When we preach the Old Testament, we must help people see and understand that, left to ourselves, we are opposed to God and resist the promises that come through His Son. In Ruth, we are the family of Elimelech, Naomi, Mahlon and Chilion who left the land of God's people and God's promise and headed for enemy territory in Moab.

When we learn to read the Old Testament in this way, we will learn to see our need for Christ and the urgency of setting our hope on Christ. We will learn to stop "applying the Bible to the 'real world'" and to begin urging people to apply themselves to the real world of the Bible. One day, things that seem very real and very important in this life will seem as nothing compared to the Son of God. When we grasp this truth, we will go to the Old Testament not for mere principles to improve our lives. We will go there to see the promised Son of God who is life.[21] As we do this, we learn to live in the present. We

---

21. Hebrews 11:1–2 makes much of "seeing" the future-coming promises of God, promises which we cannot yet see "by faith."

are able to see that in every Old Testament story and situation God is working to glorify His Son and bring Him to the nations through some of the most unlikely and undeserving people and in some of the unlikeliest of ways.

Whenever we see something we lack that God requires, we recognize it is something God supplies through His Son. The Old Testament sends us on a quest to know and find God's Son. When we do, the appropriate response is not to tweak our lives; it is to fall down at the feet of Jesus in worship and praise. The goal of preaching the Old Testament is not incrementally-improved lives; it is beholding and believing the Son. When we aim for that target, the Spirit does the rest.

THE EXAMPLE OF RUTH

We have established the Old Testament is a reliable witness to Jesus. We have presented a method for preparing Christ-centered messages from passages that directly involve God's provision of a succession of sons leading to the ultimate Son of Promise. Now we can turn to the book of Ruth and see the methodology in action.

The book of Ruth recounts the story of a family that initially abandons the land of the Lord's promises and His people because of a famine. Yet by the story's end, the family is miraculously redeemed when God provides a miracle son in Bethlehem. As we will see, there is more to the story, but that is the basic outline. A miracle son brings redemption to Naomi's family and includes a Gentile woman, Ruth the Moabitess, in this story of redemption and as a mother in the lineage of King David and, eventually, of Jesus, the King of Kings.

All of this happens in Bethlehem. During Advent, Micah 5:2 is frequently (and accurately) cited as a direct prophecy of Jesus's birth in Bethlehem. While Micah 5:2 is clear and direct evidence, Ruth also highlights God's plan to send His Promised Son to be born in Bethlehem. As we will see, by chapter 4, Ruth connects the story of the provision of God's Promised Son from Abraham to Judah, to Boaz and Obed and all the way to King David. On a first reading of the Old Testament, it may not seem that Bethlehem figures all that prominently in the story of God's redemption through His Son, but the book of Ruth suggests otherwise. In Ruth, Bethlehem of Judah is shown to stand at the center of the story of the provision of many sons who are in the genealogical line leading to the birth of David in Bethlehem.

Ruth is a book that helps us understand that in God's story what is most significant often happens in the narratives we tend to overlook. Ruth, just a few pages in the Old Testament, connects to much of what God is doing for and through His people in the world. What happens in Bethlehem must not be overlooked; indeed, it is essential to the story of the redemption of God's people. Without God's provision of a son in the house of bread (i.e. Bethlehem), the people of God would have no king in the city of peace (i.e. Jerusalem). This was true in the journey from the period of the judges to the rise of King David, and it would be true again when it seemed God's promises of a forever-King in the line of David had failed. Long after David has died, the story of Ruth beckons us to remember what God accomplished in Bethlehem. If David had come from a family line that was as good as dead, the Promised Son would surely come, and He would come from Bethlehem.

As we realize the seemingly obscure town of Bethlehem is central to God's redemption story, the Spirit opens our eyes to see other details in Ruth are guideposts pointing us to Jesus, God's ultimate redeemer. The truth that God's Redeeming Son comes "from Bethlehem" is only the beginning of what God reveals in Ruth.

Ruth not only highlights the location for the arrival of God's Redeeming Son; it also reveals the Son Himself. The Old Testament speaks about Jesus not only through direct prophecies but in the details of the stories about the featured sons of promise who are highlighted along the way to the Son of Promise. It is not accidental that Ruth is a story of a miraculous redemption through the birth of a son in Bethlehem.

Ruth is preparing us to recognize Jesus, God's Promised Son and Redeemer, who is miraculously conceived in the Virgin Mary and born in Bethlehem. Ruth is more than a short story about one family's redemption; it is a Spirit-authored story about Jesus, God's Son of Promise—a story that reveals not only where God's redeemer will be born (i.e. Bethlehem) but also who Jesus is as God's ultimate redeeming Son.

In chapter 1, we will see that redemption begins when we stop seeking our own "bread" in enemy territory and instead turn to the Lord. In chapter 2, we will see that access to the bread God provides in Bethlehem must come through a son who will graciously provide it. As Boaz welcomes Ruth to work in his field and graciously provides for her and Naomi's needs, we see a picture of Jesus who welcomes Gentiles into the family of God by offering Himself to them as the Bread of Life. In chapter 3, as Boaz faces great temptation on the threshing floor, we see a picture of Jesus who is a worthy man, a man who refused to yield to temptation so that sinners may be redeemed from sin. The need for a redeemer who is a close relative also comes into view, as we see that the incarnation of Jesus was necessary for Him to be a "near relative" or "kinsman-redeemer" for sinners. In chapter 4, multiple aspects of redemption are beautifully brought together. The refusal of another possible kinsman-redeemer demonstrates that redemption is costly, and Jesus willingly pays the price. Boaz's marriage to Ruth illustrates the intimacy of redemption in Jesus, a redemption in which He marries Himself to the church by sacrificing Himself for her good. The miraculous conception of Obed in the womb of a barren, Gentile widow helps us understand Jesus is, indeed, a son and a Savior for people from all nations. The birth of Obed in the place of Elimelech and his sons demonstrates Jesus will be a son who is born to take the place of sinners so that those who would otherwise remain dead in their trespasses and sins might be raised up to life everlasting in God's land. Finally, the concluding genealogy reminds us God's story has always been about how God keeps His promises through His Son, a Son who would rule as King. Jesus is in the text of Ruth; let's go see Him and feast upon Him there (John 6:41ff).

RUTH ONE
NO BREAD IN BETHLEHEM

When I preached through the book of Ruth, I did so during the season of Advent. To be sure, this may have seemed a bit unusual when the incarnation and birth of Jesus is so familiarly captured in the Gospels of Matthew and Luke. But, that was partly the point. I wanted to show that the gospel of redemption through God's Son is proclaimed not only in the New Testament gospels but also in the Old Testament. At Christmas, and in every season, the book of Ruth is a story of God's miraculous provision for His people through a son born in Bethlehem, and that is no accident.

As we read Ruth 1, we encounter Naomi, who fled Bethlehem during a famine, now encouraging her two widowed and childless daughters-in-law to remain in their homeland of Moab as she returns to her hometown. Naomi's reason for urging them to stay behind catches our attention—it is impossible for her to give them sons to marry and care for them. Furthermore, their lack of children suggests they have been unable to conceive (vv. 11–13). It seemed best to Naomi that Orpah and Ruth stay behind in Moab and do what they could to provide for themselves among their own people in familiar territory. If they return with her, their only hope would be that the Lord would do the impossible and provide a son in

Bethlehem in the place of Elimelech and his sons to give them life, provision, and standing in their new home and among a new people.[1]

Ruth opens with a critical and life-defining choice that will only lead to sustained blessing if God provides a son in Bethlehem. We know, because Ruth ends with the birth of a son who is in the line of Judah and a forefather of King David and of King Jesus, that God does provide such a son, but we do not know that yet. Before we arrive there, we must first consider chapter 1, a story of repentance that sets in motion God's eventual provision through the birth of an unlikely son.

The significance of the book of Ruth in previewing the story of God's provision through His Promised Son is reflected in Matthew's inclusion of Ruth in the genealogy of Jesus. His listing of Jesus's genealogy is comprised mostly of fathers and sons, but in Matthew 1:5–6, he writes, "Boaz was the father of Obed by Ruth, and Obed the father of Jesse. Jesse was the father of David the king."

There is something so significant about Ruth that Matthew includes her in his genealogy of Jesus. Within the 85 verses that comprise the book of Ruth, we find a strikingly similar story to the story of Christ's arrival in Bethlehem—a story of a childless woman who, by the end of the book, miraculously holds her son and the promise of God's salvation in her hands.

---

1. This theme will receive greater explanation in later chapters, but the book of Ruth opens with the death of sons because a son will be required to redeem Naomi and perpetuate Elimelech's family name. Ruth, as an outsider from Moab, will also need someone who is willing to welcome her into the family. Ruth will show us much about the redeeming son who comes from Bethlehem, but chapter 1 introduces the theme and then focuses on repentance by way of Naomi and Ruth "turning" to Bethlehem.

Throughout the following chapters, I will refer to sections of Ruth as scenes in a play. This is not to suggest the story of Ruth is not historical or accurate—it is. The characters are real, historical figures that God uses to portray for us the dramatic and profound nature of the redemption God's people have through Jesus Christ, His Promised Son. While I use my own title for most of the "scenes" in Ruth, I am indebted to Robert Holmstedt for his division of Ruth into "acts" and "scenes" in the dramatic unfolding of God's redemption of Ruth, Naomi, and ultimately of us through His provision of a most unlikely son.[2]

However, before we learn of God's redemption through a son, Naomi must first turn to the Lord. This is the problem and the theme of chapter 1: will anyone from the featured family turn to the Lord? Chapter 1 (Act One) is presented in three scenes. In scene 1 (vv. 1–5), we see famine, a family's departure from Bethlehem, and the calamity that comes. In scene 2 (vv. 6–19a), Naomi hears good news that bread is in Bethlehem, and Orpah ultimately stays behind in Moab while Ruth goes with Naomi to the land where God's people dwell. In scene 3 (vv. 19b–22), these two women, Naomi and Ruth, enter Bethlehem with nothing but dependence upon God "at the beginning of the barley harvest" (v. 22).

Scene One: Flight, Famine and Futility | God Wants Us to Turn to Him (vv. 1–5)

We could call the first scene (vv. 1–5), flight, famine, and futility. The major theme in this opening scene runs throughout the Scriptures and is foundational to our understanding and presentation of the gospel. To be rescued by God, we must turn not to ourselves but to the Lord as King.

---

2. Robert D. Holmstedt, *Ruth, A Handbook on the Hebrew Text*, (Waco, TX: Baylor U Press, 2010), 51ff.

Verse 1 is packed with key information. We learn the setting, the timeframe, and the problem. This story occurs, "in the days when the judges governed" (v. 1). This is the time after the Israelites enter the Promised Land but before they have a king, the period between 1250 BC and 1050 BC.[3] During this period, there are brief seasons of faithfulness when God raises up a faithful judge but mostly extended seasons of rebellion against God.[4] Judges concludes with these words, "In those days there was no king in Israel; everyone did what was right in his own eyes" (Judges 21:25).

Although Israel had been given the choicest of lands in which to obey God (e.g. "a land flowing with milk and honey" in Exod 3:17), they did exactly what Moses warned them against when he says,

> Beware that you do not forget the Lord your God by not keeping His commandments and His ordinances and His statutes which I am commanding you today; otherwise, when you have eaten and are satisfied, and have built good houses and lived in them, and when your herds and your flocks multiply, and your silver and gold multiply, and all that you have multiplies, then your heart will become proud and you will forget the Lord your God who brought you out from the land of Egypt, out of the house of slavery (Deut 8:11–14).

When God gave instructions pertaining to blessings for obedience and curses for rebellion, He was clear. If the Israelites did not obey Him, as they pledged to do, they would not flourish but would face famine. As Moses writes, "Cursed shall be your basket and your

---

3. Sinclair B. Ferguson, *Faithful God: An Exposition of the Book of Ruth*, (Bryntirion, Bridgend CF31 4DX, Wales: Bryntirion Press, 2005), 21.

4. Perhaps, most interestingly for the purposes of locating the earthly origins of God's redemption in Bethlehem is the very brief mention of the tenth judge of Israel, Izban of Bethlehem. He governs for seven years, and, unlike most other judges, has no human father listed in the text. See Judges 12:8–10.

kneading bowl. Cursed shall be the offspring of your body and the produce of your ground, the increase of your herd and the young of your flock" (Deut 28:17–18).

Like Adam and Eve in the Garden of Eden, Israel neglected God's commands and rebelled against Him, and God did as He promised. Famine came to Bethlehem.

This does not mean every famine is a sign of God's direct judgment. Famines generally happen because creation has been impacted by sin, and the curse that followed the first sin included the difficulty of obtaining bread to eat (Gen 3:17–19). However, Ruth is a story that begins in the Promised Land and involves a people who are (or at least should be) familiar with God's words regarding blessings, curses, and His use of famines to give them an opportunity to return to Him. Absent a specific command to leave the Promised Land, God intends for His people to remain in the place He gave them.[5]

The famine at the beginning of the book of Ruth is a wake-up call from the Lord, a call for His people to stop filling themselves with self and to seek their satisfaction in Him. The evidence of relying upon the Lord would be remaining in God's land. To stay would take real faith because famines are awful. As Peter Lau and Gregory Goswell note, "The book of Lamentations suggests that those who

---

5. Peter H. W. Lau and Gregory Goswell, *Unceasing Kindness: A Biblical Theology of Ruth, New Studies in Biblical Theology*, (Downers Grove, IL: InterVarsity Press, 2016), 74. Lau and Goswell note in the introduction to their chapter on Famine in Ruth that "Since there is no explicit evaluation by the narrator, interpreters are divided over how to evaluate Elimelech's decision to take his family out of the Promised Land. Some commentators view Elimelech's actions as springing from a lack of trust in God and the subsequent tragedies as God's punishment. Other commentators argue that the tragic events should be understood as incidental details that function to set the scene for the following plot" (p. 71). They conclude, after a review of other Biblical famines, that the witness of Scripture is that "the default location for God's people is the Promised Land" (p. 74).

perish by the sword are better off than those who suffer from famine. Thus, famine was the most-feared catastrophe, most likely because of the drawn out and excruciating nature of the suffering."[6]

But, if God's people will turn to Him, He will break the famine. As the Lord said through Moses in Deuteronomy 30, "return to the Lord your God...then the Lord your God...will make you abundantly prosperous in all the work of your hand, in the fruit of your womb...and in the fruit of your ground (vv. 2, 3, 9).

If God's people will heed the message of the famine, He will answer. Unfortunately, Naomi's family misses the divine memo. They do not turn to God. Instead, her husband, Elimelech, whose name means, "my God is King" does not practice what his own name should have been preaching to him. Rather than rest in God's sovereign rule, he leaves behind God's land and the people through whom God had promised to provide His King. As Sinclair Ferguson writes, "They are forsaking the only place on earth God has specifically given to His people, the place in which He has promised to bless them."[7]

It does not take much time in the Old Testament to realize many of the names have a meaning that supports the message the Lord is communicating to us. In this case, the family decides to leave behind not just any place in the Promised Land but the town of Bethlehem (literally, "house of bread").

Certainly, this family should know the God who provided manna from heaven in the wilderness can break a famine in a town called the "House of Bread." They lived in Judah (v. 1, 2), the very land

---

6. Lau and Goswell, 77.
7. Ferguson, 25

assigned to the tribe from which God had promised to raise up His Son and forever-King (Gen 49:10).

However, the arrival of a famine proves to be the tipping point for this family. Perhaps they had given up on the idea that the Lord could use any of their sons or involve them in His plan to bring salvation to His world. The professed faith of many has been shown to be lacking when adversity strikes. Namaan the leper was happy to travel to Israel for healing, but he balked at the idea of washing in the Jordan. Peter recognized Jesus as the Messiah but was subsequently rebuked by Jesus for wanting a salvation that would come without the cross. Trials either expose our faith as lacking or nonexistent, or they refine our faith. Only those who trust in the Lord can encounter a famine and "Consider it all joy...when [they] encounter various trials" (James 1:2).

In the case of Naomi and Elimelech, they had apparently faced challenging times long before the famine. Of all the names they could have chosen for their sons, they selected Malon, meaning "sickling" and Chilion, meaning "weakling."

Their hopes are supposed to be set on God's provision of His Promised Son through their very tribe. Instead, it seems they have given up hope that God sees them or would use their sons. When famine comes, they move from frustration to faithlessness. They walk away; you might say they are like their sons, sick and weak in their faith, if they ever had faith at all. To them, their desperate circumstances appear to be too daunting for their seemingly distant God. They take matters into their own hands, and they head out for Moab.[8]

---

8. Lau and Goswell in *Unceasing Kindness* (see footnote 5) write that "Since Elimelech chose to take his family out of the Promised Land, it seems likely that the food shortage affected the whole of Israel (Ruth 1:1).

Yes...Moab, that Moab! In Num 22, the King of Moab hires Balaam
to curse Israel. In Judges 3, Eglon, the fat king of Moab, defeats Israel and makes them his subjects for 18 years. When famine comes,
this family does not turn to the Lord; this family flees to enemy territory. Moab had been such a treacherous enemy of Israel that "no
Moabite was to enter the assembly of Yahweh to the tenth generation!"[9]

When they depart, they only intend to "sojourn in the land of
Moab" (v. 1). A sojourn means a short trip, but in verse 2, we read
that "they entered the land of Moab and remained there." When the
Scripture says they remained there, it means they remained there!
We read in verse 4 that they were there "about 10 years." Ten years
does not represent a sojourn; it signifies a hardened resolve to make
a new life in a new place separated from the Lord and His people.

What they initially justified as a little self-preservation was really presumption that they could live without God. What they intended as
a time out became a train wreck. As Ferguson writes, "They seek to
take the provision God promises apart from the repentance God requires."[10]

The Lord does not send or allow famine to remind us we need mere
physical food. Famine comes so we will recognize we need the One
who makes food possible more than we need food itself. Our response should be to turn to the Lord in faith. As Lau and Goswell
write, "Although there might be a famine, God can still bless abun-

---

Climatically, Moab could have received more rain than Israel because the
Transjordan plateau is higher than the Cisjordan in some sections. Hence,
rain would fall on the western margins of Moab. However, as we discussed
above, a lack of rainfall can also be interpreted theologically" (pp. 78–9).

9. James M. Hamilton Jr., *God's Glory in Salvation through Judgment: A
Biblical Theology*, (Wheaton, IL: Crossway, 2010), 309.

10. Ferguson, 25.

dantly."[11] We see this perhaps most poignantly in the story of the prodigal son who does not return to his father until "a severe famine occurred" (Luke 15:14). The famine gets the prodigal's attention. He returns home, and he finds that blessing is available on the other side of the famine because the Father is ready to welcome and receive those who come to Him in desperation and faith.

However, the famine at the beginning of our story does not drive Naomi and her family toward God. In the departure of Naomi's family for Moab, we see the prideful and self-reliant default setting of the sin-warped human heart. When famine comes, whether real or perceived, whether we lack purpose, pleasure, or physical provision, sinners naturally turn to themselves.

This is the exact opposite of what we should do. As this opening scene demonstrates, running from God when things seem hopeless is the path of hopelessness. Even in times of abundance, times when we are tempted to believe we no longer need the Lord (Deut 8:10–14), fleeing the place and the people where God has promised to make His presence known and fulfill His promises is foolish and futile.

Notice what happens to this family that flees. While in Moab, Naomi loses her husband (v. 3), and she and her sons are left all alone. Following the death of Elimelech, her sons marry, contrary to the Mosaic law, Moabite wives (v. 4). We do not know how long after Elimelech died that they are married, and we are not certain whether the clock on the ten years mentioned in verse 4 begins with the arrival of Naomi's family in Moab or with the marriage of her sons. Regardless, what we see is a deepening of Naomi's crisis. When her husband dies, her sons marry, but tragedy strikes again when

---

11. Lau and Goswell, 73.

they also die (v. 5). As Lau and Goswell write,

> Along with physical hunger, a spiritual hunger can
> be detected in the book of Ruth. Although named
> 'elîmelek, "My God is King", his departure from the
> Promised Land reflects a lack of recognition of
> God's sovereignty, of trust in God: a spiritual
> emptiness. A father's practical apostasy has physical
> outcomes—barrenness in both his sons' marriages,
> and three deaths.[12]

Naomi is without a husband and without sons. As Holmstedt writes, "In terms of plot development, the problem, No'omi's abandonment, is further complicated."[13] Every family needed a son to secure property rights in the land, continue the family name, and continue providing for the family. By verse 5, Naomi has lost her husband and her sons. The brief trip to Moab has become a series of bitter losses.

Naomi left because bread was scarce, but now her life is in jeopardy. If Naomi's story was a tragedy, this is where her story would conclude (see Matt 12:45).

The worst possible scenario is now Naomi's reality. She left because life on God's terms and in God's place seemed impossible, and now her life is impossible—unless God intervenes and gives her a son (see Gen 3:15, Luke 1:37). The people of God never find hope by running from Him.

Calamity comes when we abandon God. The bitter consequences of sin are a bit like spiritual gravity. When we rise to be our own savior, our lives come crashing down. Yet, it is precisely when we realize we

---

12. Lau and Goswell, 80.
13. Holmstedt, 64.

cannot save ourselves that we find there is an opportunity to turn to the Lord. Charles Swindoll reflects this sentiment.

> The best framework for the Lord God to do His most ideal work is when things are absolutely impossible, and we feel totally unqualified to handle it. That's His favorite circumstance. Those are His ideal working conditions.[14]

When we finally realize we are completely hopeless and helpless unless God miraculously intervenes, we find a window of hope.[15] When we finally reach the state of hopelessness, God works through our hopelessness to call us to return to Him. The question of scene 2 is this: how will Naomi and her daughters-in-law respond to the opportunity to turn to the Lord?

Scene Two: Decision Time | To turn to God, we must trust Him to provide for us against all odds (vv. 6–19a)

In verse 6, we have a sliver of hope, a light shining in the darkness. Naomi has no son, but she learns Yahweh has "visited" His people. He has cared for them by providing "food." The activity of God is evident throughout Ruth. Verse 6 is one of two places in Ruth where God is specifically said to act.[16] God broke the famine in Bethlehem for the sake of His people. There was food (literally, "bread")

---

14. Charles R. Swindoll, *Great Days with the Great Lives*, (Nashville: W Publishing Group, 2005) 76.

15. As Ruth unfolds, we will see God's miraculous intervention. He will bring life to an otherwise dead family line. He will provide bread to those who have no bread, and He will give legal standing in His land and among His people to people who would have otherwise been cut off from Him and His promises. The miraculous intervention of God on our behalf through the gift of a Son is multifaceted. Ruth highlights God's miraculous and multifaceted provision through His Son.

16. It strikes me that Ruth and Esther are similar in this way. While Ruth makes mention of God's name and Esther does not, both rely heavily

again in the House of Bread. As we also see in Luke 15, when prodigals remember there is more than enough bread in their Father's house, they have an opportunity to return. So, Naomi gets up to "return" or to turn from Moab back to the land of God's provision.

The Hebrew word *šûb* (שׁוּב), meaning "turn" or "return," occurs twelve times (1:6, 7, 8, 10, 11, 12, 15 [x2], 16, 21, 22 [x2]) in chapter 1 and occurs only three additional times in the remainder of Ruth.[17] Clearly, chapter 1 is about a turn or a change, not just in physical location but from self-reliance to relying on the Lord. We are on solid ground in this interpretation of Ruth 1 because *šûb* is also the Hebrew word for repentance—to turn away from the worship of self and other idols and to the worship of God.

The author of Ruth uses a spatial term (*šûb*) to communicate a spiritual reality.[18] To return to the land of Judah is to return to the place of God's people, His presence, His promises, and His provision which will ultimately come through His promised Son and King. Chapter 1 of Ruth is about the need for repentance, for being converted, for turning to God.

Will Naomi go back to Bethlehem with no husband and no sons and fully rely on God to give her daily bread? How will she have daily bread without a son to secure her inheritance in the land? Will her daughters-in-law turn away from Moab and return with Naomi? In turning to Bethlehem, Naomi provides a living illustra-

---

on things that happen to indicate that the Sovereign Lord is at work to save His people.

17. Lau and Goswell, 80.

18. The use of physical or spatial language to communicate a spiritual reality is common in Scripture. The use of "return" (*šûb*) in this way helps us see that the presence or lack of bread functions in a similar way in the story. A famine (v. 1) leads to a lack of bread, but God breaks the famine as a direct act of "visiting" or caring for His people and providing them bread (v. 6). In verse 6, Naomi considers returning because there is bread.

tion of the Lord's prayer. Her only hope is that the Lord would supply her with daily bread.

As we encounter Naomi's decision to return, we have no indication there is a famine in Moab. Presumably, she still has bread in Moab, but aside from having physical bread to eat, her life in Moab has been "a place of death and bitterness."[19] Her journey back to Bethlehem is an admission that life is about more than having physical bread.[20] Naomi has seen the consequences of leaving the Lord, and she is ready to humbly return and seek His provision.

In verse 7, they all set out to return to the land of Judah. Of course, Orpah and Ruth were not really returning because they had never been to Judah. However, they were turning from their foreign gods and trusting in God alone—or so it seemed.

Everything suggests a routine and uneventful trip in verse 7, and then we encounter verse 8. There is no indication of how far down the road the women have traveled. We do not know if they stopped for lunch or a bathroom break. Perhaps, there was just a strange feeling that not everyone was on board with this trip to Bethlehem. Whatever the reason, it was time for a serious conversation.

In verses 8–9, Naomi says (my paraphrase), "Look, I've told you about my Lord. Go home, find some new husbands, and may the

---

Although she has neither a son nor standing in the land, she returned from Moab to Bethlehem, the House of Bread, at the "beginning of barley harvest" (v. 22). God's provision is always available when we turn to Him.

19. Laura A. Smit and Stephen E. Fowl, *Judges and Ruth, The Brazos Theological Commentary on the Bible*, (Grand Rapids: Brazos, 2018), 219.

20. This point is clear not only by way of the symbolism employed in Ruth but in other books as well. Consider how the presence/absence of bread is used in the book of Lamentations to reflect the distance of God's people from their land and from the Lord (Lam 1:11; 2:12; 5:6, 9).

Lord deal kindly with you as you have with me, and may He give you rest." In Hebrew, the word "deal kindly" is *hesed* (חסד), a word that refers to the covenant faithfulness of God toward His people. When it is used to speak of human relationships, it refers to mercy or kindness that goes beyond what is required. Orpah and Ruth had demonstrated such kindness to the dead—likely a reference to "physically caring for the bodies and preparing them for the grave"—and to Naomi as well.[21] Take note of this word now. It will be important in the chapters yet to come. God will indeed show His *hesed*, and He will do it through the *hesed* of a man who is qualified to give life to those who turn to the Lord.

In verses 9–10, Orpah and Ruth weep and refuse Naomi's command. So, in verse 11, Naomi repeats the command and makes her case, and as she does, she shows us "the cost of discipleship."[22] Consider Ferguson's words about discipleship from his exposition of verses 9–10. He writes:

> Naomi is doing what she has probably never done, indeed, could not have done, in Moab. She is speaking about what may be involved in yielding to the grace of God. Nothing will be guaranteed to us except that his grace will be sufficient for all our needs, and that he will never be our debtor. There is no promise of financial security, far less material prosperity. God does not guarantee our comfort. That is why the new Naomi is inviting her daughters-in-law to count the cost of belonging to the Lord. It might well mean: no husband; no guaranteed provision or security; no children; no human hope.[23]

---

21. Smit and Fowl, 220.
22. Ferguson, 30.
23. Ferguson, 31.

Turning to God means following Him no matter the hardships we must surely face. When we run away from God in response to the difficulties that come in life, we compromise our ability to credibly call on others to follow Christ. However, Naomi is now turning to the Lord, no matter the costs, no matter the embarrassment that awaits her in Bethlehem, and now she speaks truth to her daughters-in-law.

Naomi will go to Bethlehem where she will have no husband to provide for her needs and no son to secure her property or perpetuate the family name. She is too old to have sons, and even if she could, it would be ridiculous for Orpah and Ruth to "refrain from marrying" or literally "imprison" (v. 13) themselves by having no husband.

Besides the lack of the availability of husbands for Orpah and Ruth and Naomi's lack of a son, Naomi says the overall bitterness or hardness of life that awaits her is something she does not want them to share.[24]

Once the costs of turning to the Lord are recounted, we see in the responses of Orpah and Ruth (vv. 14–18) the difference between worldly and godly sorrow, between regret and repentance (see 2 Cor 7:10). When Orpah hears of the costs of going to Bethlehem, she kisses Naomi goodbye, and is never mentioned in the story again. When people reject their need to turn to the Lord and embrace a new life with His people, they end up missing out on being a part of God's story. Ruth, however, "clings" to Naomi as a husband clings to his wife (Gen 2:24). As Steven Fowl writes, "Ruth is forging a bond with Naomi, her people, and her God that only death can break."[25]

---

24. Holmstedt, 84.
25. Smit and Fowl, 222.

Orpah and Ruth have both wept twice (vv. 9, 14), but they weep for different reasons. Orpah regrets that she will not see Naomi again, that things have not gone as she hoped. But when Ruth weeps, she weeps tears of conviction (see 2 Cor 7:10). She will join God's people and trust Him no matter what it costs. This is Ruth's profession of faith, her conversion. She believes God will provide for her even though it is humanly impossible. Not only is she without a husband or a son, she is not even an Israelite!

So, in verse 15, Naomi says to Ruth (my paraphrase), "See there! Orpah turned to her people and her gods; you go do the same." Ruth responds in verses 16–17 (again, my paraphrase), "Stop it! You will not talk me out of this. I am going with you. I am remaining with you. I am not turning back to the gods of my ancestors. I am not turning to Moab; I am turning to the God of your people. Your God will be my God. I will be buried in your land in anticipation of the resurrection that is to come through your people."

How do we explain Ruth's confidence and conviction? Ultimately, it is a picture of the sort of confidence God produces in the heart of a genuine child of God. I suspect Ruth had heard somehow, despite the mostly negative example of Naomi's life to this point, of the one true God.

Perhaps she had heard the story of the Moabite King who hired Balaam to curse Israel. But when Balaam tried repeatedly to curse Israel, the Lord prevented him, and eventually he declared, "I see him, but not now; I behold him, but not near; a star shall come forth from Jacob, a scepter shall rise from Israel, and shall crush through the forehead of Moab....One from Jacob shall have dominion" (Num 24:17, 19a).

We cannot know for sure how Ruth came to have such confidence in the Lord, but we know God did not waste Naomi's disobedience. God allows Naomi's painful time in Moab to lead to Ruth's great salvation—and, as we will see, to our salvation as well. By verse 18, Naomi is convinced that Ruth is convinced. She says nothing more (v. 18), and these two sonless widows return to Bethlehem (v. 19a). Both women finished their journey to the place where their only hope for life was that God would provide against all odds.

Scene Three: Entering Bethlehem | When those who are empty turn to the Lord, God gives a harvest (vv. 19b–22)

Naomi returns to Bethlehem, and it stirs up "all the city" (v. 19). Ferguson sees in verse 19 the reality that, "It takes only one conversion for a church to begin to believe again in the regenerating power of God. The impact of one individual coming to faith can transform the whole community."[26]

What does it take for you or your church to be stirred up? Meeting the budget is great. Renovating and constructing a new facility is great. But what should truly stir us up is repentance. As Jesus says, "there will be more joy in heaven over one sinner who repents than over ninety-nine righteous persons who need no repentance" (Luke 15:7). Perhaps you know such a person. Perhaps you have been such a person. Perhaps God is leading you to pray for such a person.

Naomi was such a person. She had been away from the people of God and the place of God's provision for at least a decade and likely longer. She had left for a sojourn that ended up severing her from God's people and His provision. Long before she had been short on

---

26. Ferguson, 37.

physical bread, she had been missing out on knowing and trusting God her provider.

Imagine the city looking on and word spreading as they see Naomi walking into the city with no husband, no sons, and a young woman from Moab. Could this really be Naomi? Certainly, time and tears had taken their toll on her appearance.

The women of the city understandably ask, "Is this Naomi?" Is the woman we had long since assumed we would never see again really standing before us? When the women ask their question, Naomi is ready with her confession, "No, I am not Naomi (a name which means 'pleasant'); instead, call me Mara (a name meaning 'bitter')" (v. 20).

With these words, Naomi is saying (my paraphrase), "I have endured a great deal. I left Bethlehem and the promises of God, and when you do that, the Almighty allows you to reap the bitter consequences. The Lord took me to court, and He witnessed against me. He is right. I am bitter and guilty, and He is my only hope (v. 21)."

Naomi wants to be called Mara so, as Ferguson puts it, her "life may be a standing testimony to the way in which God brings the sweet out of the bitter, and gives his grace in the midst of our sin and failure."[27] Naomi is essentially saying, "Look, when I left, I was full. I had a full family, a family full of determination to make our own success in the world. Now, I know the bitter emptiness that comes when our lives are filled by anything other than the Lord. When there was a famine, I was pleasantly full of myself, but I have known the bitter disappointment of self-trust and have returned humble and destitute—'empty'" (v. 21).

---

27. Ferguson, 36.

Now that Naomi has returned empty, there is finally room for God to fill her. Verse 22 concludes the first act in a way that suggests God's provision is indeed on the way. For in Bethlehem, it is the "beginning of barley harvest."

We have not yet seen how Naomi will come to have a share in God's provision, but the progress of the chapter strongly suggests the Lord will provide—both for Naomi and for Ruth.

Naomi's husband has died. Her sons have died. Ruth has left all earthly security to be joined to Naomi's God and her people. These women are empty, and when empty people turn to the Lord, He provides.

God does not fill people who are full of themselves, but He has more than enough spiritual bread for people who come to Him empty.[28] If you are empty, frustrated, sick, and tired of trying to do for yourself what only God can do in and for you, it is time to turn from your sin and turn to the Lord who gives bread in Bethlehem.

To understand how God will provide for Naomi and Ruth, we must keep reading. But for now, we trust the implicit promise of verse 22; it is the beginning of barley harvest, and God finishes what He starts (see Phil 1:6).

We know God finishes what He starts because He sent His Son who declared from the cross, "It is finished" (John 19:30). God sent His Son to a world starved for His presence because of their sin. This Son would be broken to forgive our sins and to fill us, not with mere bread, but with life everlasting in Himself. It is no accident that

---

28. Consider using the parable of the prayers of the Pharisee and tax collector to illustrate this point (Luke 18:9–14).

Jesus, the Bread of Life, is born in Bethlehem, the House of Bread. All the hope and promise of Ruth is fulfilled when the promised Son of God who brings ultimate redemption and deliverance to God's people comes. God does provide a Son, and He is our daily bread. In Jesus, we have the "bread" which truly satisfies. Consider that centuries after this story, Mary, while anticipating the birth of Jesus, declares "[The Lord] has filled the hungry with good things" (Luke 1:53).

If you are hungry, leave your sinful self-reliance and stubborn insistence on your own way behind, and turn to the Lord. Jesus was born in Bethlehem to die for your sins and to be raised to give you a new life in Him. If you are empty, come to Jesus and be filled. The bread you really need comes from Bethlehem.

QUESTIONS FOR PASTORS AND TEACHERS

1. What is the significance of the mention of famine and departure (v. 1) and then return and harvest (v. 22) at the beginning and end of the chapter?

2. What other famines occur in Scripture, and how do they bear on our understanding of the famine at the beginning of Ruth? (The chapter by Peter Lau and Gregory Goswell is an excellent resource).[29]

3. Is there any significance to the reality that the death of Naomi's husband and sons precedes her hearing of the good news that the Lord had visited His people (v. 6)? Can we say that the death of her sons leads her to consider that true life comes from the Lord which He later (in chapter 4) provides them through

---

29. Peter H. W. Lau and Gregory Goswell, *Unceasing Kindness: A Biblical Theology of Ruth, New Studies in Biblical Theology*, (Downers Grove, IL: InterVarsity Press, 2016), 71ff.

the birth of an unlikely son? Can we say that God saves Naomi through the death and birth of a son of Judah?

4. How will I use the comparison and contrast of the responses of Orpah and Ruth to challenge my church to examine themselves to see that they are in the faith...to ensure they are clinging to Christ and truly following Him?

5. How much should I emphasize that Ruth is called "the Moabitess" and connect this with the opportunity for Gentiles to be saved and become a part of God's people in chapter 1? This theme will appear again in chapter 2.

SMALL-GROUP DISCUSSION QUESTIONS

1. Why do natural disasters occur in the world today?

2. When disaster strikes, should we assume the disaster is an act of direct judgment against the sins of the people impacted by the disaster? How might Jesus's response to His disciples in John 9:3 help us?

3. What trials have you faced that God has used to help strengthen and refine your faith in Him?

4. Why can't people fill themselves spiritually?

5. What are the dangers of "taking a break" from your local church? How is this like a sojourn in Moab?

6. When did you first recognize the emptiness of trusting in yourself and turning to God for the spiritual food that only He can provide?

7. When Naomi turns away from Moab and back to Bethlehem, she brings Ruth with her. Who did you (or could you) bring with you to become a part of God's people?

8. When Ruth decides to stay with Naomi and leave behind everything she has known, do you think she loved Naomi or Naomi's God? Why is this question important for us?

9. God used Naomi's pain to bring Ruth into His family. When has God worked through your difficult circumstances (or perhaps the circumstances of another believer) to bring someone else closer to Him?

10. Where do we find Ruth's profession of faith in this chapter? Why did going to Judah with Naomi require courageous faith in the Lord?

11. Can you share about a time you did something that required courageous faith in the Lord?

12. How does Naomi's return impact the town of Bethlehem? What does this mean for the local church today?

13. What other times in Scripture (before the incarnation and birth of Jesus) can you think of that required God to miraculously provide for His people to be rescued? How do these stories heighten our anticipation for what is to come?

Ruth Two

THE REDEEMER WHO GIVES BREAD

In chapter 1, we saw the story of a family who fled Bethlehem and the land of God's people to pursue provisions in Moab. Rather than take refuge in the Lord, they left for a quick fix, abandoning the people and place of God's promises and everlasting provision to come through His Son.[1] Though they lived in Bethlehem and were of the tribe of Judah from which God had promised a forever-King (Gen 49:8–10), they left. After a decade (or perhaps more) in Moab, Naomi has found physical bread, but she has not found the "abundant life" that comes to those who trust God will provide for His people through His promised Son (John 10:10). Her experience is "bitter" because her husband and two sons die, leaving her childless (1:6).

Ruth 1 demonstrates we need more than mere bread to have true life. As Jesus says, "Man shall not live on bread alone, but on every word that proceeds out of the mouth of God.'" (Matt 4:4; cf Deut 8:3). We do not just need bread; we need bread on God's terms.

Even after Naomi hears of bread in Bethlehem, she has little reason

---

1. See Psalm 2:12.

to return other than that she is finally hungry for more than mere bread. She is turning to the Lord and His promises. If He can bring bread back to Bethlehem, perhaps He will overcome the bitterness of life she has encountered since abandoning Him.

In strictly human terms, Naomi has no reason to return. She has no husband to provide for her and no sons to continue the family name or secure her property rights. She does not even have a consistent and reliable source of daily bread.

Though faced with seemingly insurmountable odds, Naomi returns. Ruth, one of her widowed, Moabitess daughters-in-law (v. 2) follows her to Bethlehem, and this book ends up bearing her name. The other daughter-in-law, Orpah, does not follow Naomi, and she never again appears in God's story. Ruth is showing us that turning to the Lord and His people makes a forever-difference in whether you have a forever-place in God's story. Chapter 2 begins to show us how God brings His redemption to those who turn to Him.

When Naomi and Ruth arrive in Bethlehem, "it is the beginning of barley harvest" (1:22). The Lord gives bread to His people in Bethlehem, but how Naomi or Ruth will access the Lord's provision remains to be seen. Chapter 1 leaves us with the question of how Naomi and Ruth will survive and have a standing in the land without a husband or a son. How will the good news of bread in Bethlehem become good news for these two widows who have no reliable access to the bread God is providing?[2]

---

2. The answer, as we will see later in the story, is that secure access to God's provision will come through the miraculous birth of a son who rescues both Ruth and Naomi. One of the challenges of preaching Ruth is that really doing it justice requires multiple messages, but we need to understand each message in light of the story's conclusion. The birth of Obed to bring redemption to both Ruth and Naomi and ultimately to people

As we examine chapter 2, it is again helpful to view the story as unfolding something like the second act in a four-act play. Like chapter 1, it has three scenes. In scene 1, the narrator introduces us to Boaz, and Ruth happens upon his field (vv. 1–3). In scene 2, Ruth meets Boaz, and Boaz provides for her needs (vv. 4–17). In scene 3, Ruth returns to Naomi and shares grain with her from Boaz's field (vv. 18–23).[3] Let's see what we can glean from this text.

Scene 1: Ruth happens upon Boaz's field | We must recognize our need for God's grace (vv. 1–3)

Verse 1 is packed with information about this man God uses to redeem both Ruth and Naomi. How that happens remains to be seen, but to understand chapter 2, we need to realize the Spirit is beginning to paint a picture through Boaz of God's Promised Son—the ultimate redeemer who comes from Bethlehem. The language of verse 1 helps us arrive at this conclusion. The possibility of Boaz's relationship to Naomi's deceased husband is introduced, and more significantly at this point in the story, Boaz is described as "a man of great wealth" (v. 1). Some translations put it, "a worthy man." Literally, he is "a man, a mighty one of wealth/power/character."[4] As Robert Holmstedt notes:

---

from all nations is critical for understanding that the author of Ruth is using the combination of Boaz and Obed to illustrate for us what God's Promised Son will be like. The Promised Son is one who is miraculously born in Bethlehem in the line of Judah and of David, one who is a near enough relative (i.e. a human) to redeem us, one who has ample resources to provide for all who come to Him, and one who marries Himself to those He redeems.

3. In this division of the scenes, I differ slightly with Holmstedt (I am mostly following his divisions overall). In this case, I begin scene 3 in v. 17, but he begins it in v. 18.

4. Robert D. Holmstedt, *Ruth, A Handbook on the Hebrew Text*, (Waco, TX: Baylor U Press, 2010), 105.

> It is not clear which meaning of [*gibbôr*] is intended
> by the narrator. As the narrative unfolds, Boaz is
> characterized as all three: he is clearly a wealthy
> landowner; he has social power, and he is a man of
> great character. It is likely that the narrator intended
> all three and thus chose the polyvalent word to
> foreshadow what the audience will learn and to
> heighten the anticipation of a quick and happy
> outcome for No'omi.[5]

While all the senses of *gibbôr* (גבור) likely apply to Boaz, it is helpful to note that, *gibbôr* is used not only to describe people but also to describe the Lord. In Psalm 24, the Lord is described as *gibbôr* (v. 8 [x2]) in a passage which prophetically portrays the Son of God returning to heaven and entering the Father's heavenly presence after victoriously waging war against sin and death and being raised and exalted and given the Name above all other names (i.e. "Lord", Phil 2:9–11).

In Psalm 45, God is clearly King because His throne is forever (v. 6), and yet, the Psalm likewise portrays a man who is blessed by God forever (v. 2) as God's forever-King and the Lord. We have in Psalm 45 the promise of the incarnation of God's Son, the King of nations. As the psalm unfolds, the daughters of the nations are portrayed as those who, as Ruth has done in chapter 1, "forget [their] people and [their] father's house" (v. 10) and come to this King as "their Lord" (v. 11). This is significant because in Psalm 45:3, this Lord and King is called a *gibbôr*. The Lord and King who is blessed forever by God has a full share in what exclusively is God's. He has a full share in the wealth/power/character of the Lord. When Boaz is called a *gibbôr*, we are provided with a picture of God's ultimate *gibbôr*, the one of whom Isaiah says, "For unto us a child is born, unto us a son is given; and the government shall be upon his shoulder: and his name shall

---

5. Holmstedt, 105.

be called Wonderful, Counsellor, Mighty [*gibbôr*] God, Everlasting Father, Prince of Peace" (Isaiah 9:6).

In the Hebrew text of Ruth 2:1, Boaz's name comes at the end of the sentence. This builds our expectancy for encountering this man in the story. Who is this man? Will he rescue Naomi and Ruth? Will he be the son the Lord uses to get the bread of His provision to these women? Boaz is not merely a man of wealth, power, and character. He will be revealed as a relative on her deceased husband's side of the family as the chapter unfolds. Could it be that simple? Naomi and Ruth turn to Bethlehem; it happens to be the beginning of barley harvest, and there is a wealthy, powerful, and noble man who meets God's requirements for redeeming Naomi? In Leviticus 25:25, we learn that the right of redemption, of paying the price necessary to secure the land and standing of someone in Naomi's position among God's people, belonged to the "nearest relative." Will Boaz be this man?

At this point in the story, we know about Boaz, but Naomi and Ruth do not. In verse 2, Ruth asks to glean, and Naomi agrees.[6] As Ferguson reminds us, "God had made a law about gleaning."[7] In the Law of Moses, God established gleaning.

> Now when you reap the harvest of your land, you shall not reap to the very corners of your field, nor shall you gather the gleanings of your harvest...you shall leave them for the needy and for the stranger. I am the Lord your God (Lev 19:9–10; cf Lev 23:22, Deut 24:19).

---

6. Holmstedt, 108. Holmstedt notes, "The fact the (sic) No'omi's response to Ruth is instructive suggests Ruth was in fact seeking her permission."

7. Sinclair B. Ferguson, *Faithful God: An Exposition of the Book of Ruth*, (Bryntirion, Bridgend CF31 4DX, Wales: Bryntirion Press, 2005), 51.

God commands landowners to leave the margins of their field to provide for the marginalized among them. Nevertheless, gleaning was difficult and unpredictable, depending on variables outside the control of the gleaner (i.e. the size of the margin of the field left unharvested and the number of gleaners in the field). The famine is over, but these destitute widows have no male support or claim to ancestral land and "are left to the mercy of landowners."[8]

These women need someone who will give them bread, and they need someone who will give them legal standing among the people of God. They need a man who is related to Naomi's husband, Elimelech, with the resources and the willingness to redeem them ("one of our redeemers," v. 20).[9] However, their immediate need is bread.

Ruth sets out in obedience to God's laws of gleaning, but she does not do so presumptively. She is not looking for any random field with grain but for "one in whose sight I may find favor" (v. 2). Favor is the word for grace. Ruth is not seeking a god who helps those who helps themselves; she seeks the God who generously and lavishly rescues the hopeless. She needs someone who is qualified to give her help and willing to intervene in her desperate situation. She is, after all, a barren widow from Moab. While the law provided for a way for aliens to join God's people (Num 15:14–16), Moab was among the least likely candidates. As Deuteronomy 23:3–4 says,

> No Ammonite or Moabite shall enter the assembly
> of the Lord; none of their descendants, even to the

---

8. Peter H. W. Lau and Gregory Goswell, *Unceasing Kindness: A Biblical Theology of Ruth*, New Studies in Biblical Theology, (Downers Grove, IL: InterVarsity Press, 2016), 120.

9. Jesus does all these things. He nourishes His people spiritually. He substitutes Himself for them to cancel the debt of their sin and give them legal standing among God's people (i.e. justification). He leaves heaven to be a human such that he is qualified to offer us redemption in His sacrificial death (i.e. by His blood).

tenth generation, shall ever enter the assembly of the Lord, because they did not meet you with food and water on the way when you came out of Egypt, and because they hired against you Balaam the son of Beor from Pethor of Mesopotamia, to curse you.

Verse 2 marks the third of six times Ruth is identified as a Moabitess. In Ruth 1:4, her foreign status, along with that of Orpah, is noted. Then, Ruth is identified as being from Moab in 1:22, 2:2, 2:6, 2:21, 4:5, and 4:10.[10] Ruth needs abundant grace to be joined to God's people, the sort of grace that can turn a Jacob into Israel. Ruth, like all of us, needs a way to change categories.[11]

Ruth sets out to glean, fully aware of her need for the grace of God, and she just so "happened" to enter Boaz's field. As Ferguson notes on verse 3, "more literally translated, the words are something like this: 'the happenstance that happened to her was....'"[12] When we rely on God, "happenstances happen" because God is sovereign even in the seeming coincidences of life, and He delights in rescuing those who need Him.[13] As we read in Psalm 72:12, "For He will deliver the needy when he cries for help, The afflicted also, and him who has no helper."

Ruth is new to Bethlehem and does not know what field she "happened" upon, but she is about to learn! In every story of God's rescue, note the happenstances. Note the unexpected connection, the chance meeting on an airplane, and a multitude of other things that "just happened." Ruth is showing us that it is God who is "behind the scenes" in the everyday happenstances of life leading people to

---

10. Holmstedt, 106.
11. E.g. John 3:3, 7; 2 Cor 5:17; Eph 2:1–10; Eph 4:22–24; Col 3:1–11.
12. Ferguson, 49.
13. Ferguson, 49.

His gracious provision for them in His Son.[14]

The reality is we are all like Naomi and Ruth. There is no one who does not need to be rescued and to receive life through the Son who supplies His gracious provision. As Lau and Goswell note:

> We may or may not be enslaved to material poverty, but the New Testament makes it clear that we are all slaves to sin, which leads to death (e.g. Rom 5:12; 6:16–20, 23)...Just like Ruth and Naomi and the family line of Elimelech, we need someone to intervene to redeem us.[15]

That someone is Jesus. He is the greater Boaz.[16] He is not just a man of great wealth and prominence but of infinite wealth and perfect character. Jesus is the one who has all the resources necessary to overcome your status as an outsider and welcome you to the family of God. The connections between Boaz and Jesus only grow as we read of Ruth's first meeting with Boaz in scene 2.

Scene 2: Meeting Boaz | We must behold God's redeemer and receive His bread (vv. 4–16)

Verse 4 opens with the words, "Now behold, Boaz" or "Look, Boaz!" The reader of the story finally meets the character verse 1 anticipates, and we are asked to behold him.[17] In both his identity as a

---

14. Lau and Goswell, 105.

15. Lau and Goswell, 122.

16. For an excellent explanation of why it is right to view Boaz as a type of Christ, see Lau and Goswell, 136–139.

17. For the purposes of sermon writing or lesson development, as I was meditating on chapter 2, God brought the words, "Behold Boaz" prominently to my mind. Those words framed my approach to this scene in the story. In beholding Boaz, we can see our Savior and God's Promised Son as well. I hope this section will encourage you to see and worship Christ from the Old Testament.

near relative (spelled out in chapter 3) and in his initial actions in chapter 2, we behold not merely Boaz but a picture of God's Son the ultimate redeemer from Bethlehem. In beholding Boaz, we see the amazing grace God gives through this man and a picture of the grace to come in Christ.

As we consider Boaz's lavish provision for Ruth, we are reminded of Christ's even more lavish provision for us—fullness of joy in the presence of God, direct access to the Father through Him, forevermore. Let's behold Boaz!

Behold the Redeemer who Comes from Bethlehem (v. 4)

The first thing we see in verse 4 is that Boaz, like Jesus, "came from Bethlehem," and that is only the beginning of the correspondence between Boaz and Jesus. Boaz is good to all the servants who labor in His field. He desires the Lord's presence with everyone who reaps in his field, and they desire blessing for him. This is a picture of the way Christ views the church, and the way the church views Christ. We work in His field and for His glory "because He first loved us" (1 John 4:19). Boaz provides for us a picture of the coming Son of God born in Bethlehem; He loves the laborers in His field, and His laborers love Him.

Behold the Redeemer Who Notices those in Need (v. 5)

In verse 5, after greeting the reapers in his field, the first thing Boaz notices is Ruth. She had hoped for someone to notice her in verse 2, and Boaz does precisely that in verse 5. After his customary greetings, the first thing he says is, "This girl belongs to *whom* (emphasis his)?!"[18] A young woman has come out to glean in his field, and he immediately notices. To whom does she belong? Does she not have a husband? Does she have no family to provide for her? Like Jesus, Boaz notices those who come to Him for help and healing—those who come recognizing their need for His provision. Because Jesus is God, there is always room for another laborer in His field. There are always enough resources available to provide all that is necessary for one more sinner who repents. In Mark's Gospel, the crowds are often represented as those who come to Jesus more for a show than for Him, but in Mark 8:1–3, we read:

> In those days, when there was again a large crowd and they had nothing to eat, Jesus called His disciples and said to them, "I feel compassion for the people because they have remained with Me now three days and have nothing to eat. If I send them away hungry to their homes, they will faint on the way; and some of them have come from a great distance."

As we continue reading in Mark 8, we learn that Jesus, out of His compassion, miraculously feeds the 4,000 people with just seven loaves of bread. Like Boaz, Jesus notices those who need His provision and offers them His bread.

Behold the Redeemer Who Welcomes the Outsider (vv. 6–7)

In verse 6, an underlying tension comes to the surface. The "foreman" of the field does not know what to do with the "foreigner."[19] He never even voices Ruth's name. She is "the young Moabite woman who returned with Naomi from the land of Moab" (v. 6). In verse 7, the foreman's speech is broken, communicating his nervous-

---

18. Holmstedt, 114.
19. Ferguson, 52.

ness over the situation. He says, "she entered and stood, from then—the morning—until now, this...her sitting...the house...a little."[20]

Essentially, the foreman of the field is saying, "What do I do Boaz? Should I let her glean? You do realize that she is [gasp] from Moab! What about your reputation? What will people say? I mean, do you know how long it has taken for people to accept that your mother is Rahab (Matt 1:5)?"

Verses 6-7 amplify our appreciation for Boaz and the salvation God brings to Ruth and Naomi through him. Like Jesus, Boaz welcomes the foreigner into his field. Those who are strangers, aliens, and even enemies are welcomed into the family of God through the provision of God in His Son. In Ephesians 2:1–10, the apostle Paul says people who were formerly "sons of disobedience" (v. 2) and "children of wrath" (v. 3) can be saved through Jesus. In 2 Corinthians 5:17, we see that those who were once enemies of God are "a new creature" in Christ. This is the miracle of the new birth in Christ, something Jesus calls being "born again" in John 3:1–10. When those who are outside of the family of God come to the son who offers God's redemption, they get a new identity. They are "no longer strangers and aliens, but...fellow citizens with the saints, and are of God's household" (Eph 2:19). We see this transformation of Ruth's status from foreigner to a member of the family of God in what Boaz says of her. Our redemption is not found in what others say about us, or even what we say about ourselves—it comes in what the One who is qualified to redeem us says of us.

---

20. Holmstedt, 111, 117.

Notice what Boaz says. He does not call Ruth a Moabite, but "his daughter" (v. 8).[21] He puts his reputation on the line and welcomes the outcast, the foreigner, the sinner, the one who does not belong. Likewise, Jesus risked His reputation to befriend "tax collectors and sinners" (Matt 11:19) and give them an opportunity to become the children of God. This is a picture of what Jesus does. As Peter says, "Once you were not a people, but now you are the people of God; once you had not received mercy, but now you have received mercy" (1 Pet 2:10). John puts it this way, "See how great a love the Father has bestowed on us, that we would be called children of God; and such we are" (1 John 3:1a). In a book that stresses that Ruth is from Moab, Boaz calls her "daughter." When sinners come to Christ, they are aware of their past, but they are gloriously freed of its power, and it no longer defines them.

When we arrive at the New Testament, we should not be surprised to see Gentiles welcomed into the family of God through Christ the "true vine" (John 15:1). Through faith in God's Promised Son and Redeemer, Jew and Gentile alike are the "Israel of God" (Gal 6:16). Apart from faith in God's Promised Son and Redeemer, there are no people of God. We know Jesus came to save Gentiles and include them among God's people because God promises to include people from all nations in His forever-family from the outset. In the Garden of Eden, Adam and Eve were commanded to fill the world with worshipers. They failed, and the remainder of the Scripture is a story of how God will do through His Son what Adam and his descendants failed to do—fill the world with people who are able to worship God in Spirit and truth because they have been given a new identity through Jesus Christ God's Son. In Isaiah 49:6, the Lord says:

---

21. Naomi has also called Ruth a daughter (2:2), but at this point, Naomi has no standing in the land that will help Ruth, even if she is "a daughter."

> It is too small a thing that You should be My Servant to raise up the tribes of Jacob and to restore the preserved ones of Israel; I will also make You a light of the nations so that My salvation may reach to the end of the earth.

Ruth comes to the field as a Moabitess lacking any standing among God's people, but when she encounters Boaz, she becomes his daughter. In Ruth, the Lord wants us to behold the redeemer who welcomes those who were far from God as members of God's family.

Behold the Redeemer Who Gives Abundant Grace (vv. 8–9a)

Taken together, we see in verses 8–9a, the heart of Bethlehem's redeemer in welcoming the foreigner as a daughter. As Holmstedt observes, Boaz gives:

> ...a set of instructions that go well beyond what would have been normal for gleaning. Instead of allowing Ruth to spend time in his field looking for remnant grain in the areas that had already been harvested, he urges her to "stick close to" and "follow right behind" his female harvesters....Ruth will get the first pick of the remnants since she is being allowed to follow the harvesters so closely.[22]

The intentionality of Boaz in securing ongoing and privileged access to his field reminds us of Jesus who promises, "I am the Bread of Life; he who comes to Me will not hunger, and he who believes in Me will never thirst" (John 6:35).

---

22. Holmstedt, 121.

Behold the Redeemer who Protects those Who Come to Him (v. 9b)

In verse 9b, Boaz continues, "Ruth, when you are thirsty, do not fear getting water because I have provided not only for your food but also for your protection. None of my servants will take advantage of you" (my paraphrase).

Is this not a picture of the salvation God gives in Christ? In Christ, not even the gates of hell will prevail against us (Matt 16:18). As Jesus says, "My sheep hear My voice, and I know them, and they follow Me; and I give eternal life to them, and they will never perish; and no one will snatch them out of My hand" (John 10:27–28).

What confidence we have as those who have been given the privilege of harvesting in God's field! As God sends us out to those who need to hear of the redeeming grace that we have found in Jesus, He keeps us. This does not guarantee that we will not die physically in serving Christ; it means, even if we die, we will live (e.g. John 11:25). For, as Peter says, in Christ we "are protected by the power of God through faith for a salvation ready to be revealed in the last time" (1 Pet 1:5). In the meantime, we, like Ruth, enter our redeemer's field, and we work with confidence, knowing that even as we are sent out like lambs among wolves, He will protect us as we share the gospel and harvest in His field (e.g. Luke 10:1–3ff).

Behold the Redeemer who Claims Us as His Own (v. 8)

Look carefully again at verse 8. Boaz says, "Do not go to glean in another field; furthermore, do not go on from this one." The redeemer gives bread, but he expects loyalty. Likewise, when we come to Jesus, we do not come with a plan B. When we come to Jesus, we, like Ruth, must remain in our Redeemer's field. Redemption through

God's Promised Son must come only as God's Promised Son instructs. God does not rescue us through the gift of His Son to roam around looking for food in any other field. This is known as the exclusivity of the gospel. We either have life in God's Promised Son, or we do not have true life. Spiritually speaking, our bread must be gleaned exclusively in His field. As Jesus says, "I am the way, and the truth, and the life; no one comes to the Father but through Me" (John 14:6). Those who are rescued by Jesus will devote their lives to laboring for Jesus and relying only upon His provision for their lives.

This divine provision is a wonderful and liberating truth. When we come to God's Promised Son for redemption, for rescue from our sin, we do not need to look anywhere else. Everything we are not and need, Christ is and gives. Boaz does not limit Ruth to his field to deny her something she could otherwise have; he limits her to his field because he has everything she truly needs. Anywhere else that promises bread is a delusion; it will not ultimately satisfy.

Boaz's provision and protection are available only in Boaz's field, and God's provision and everlasting life are available only in Christ. Jesus was not born in Bethlehem to offer Himself as our true bread from heaven only to receive our half-hearted devotion. He came to rescue sinners and produce within us grateful hearts that delight in Him. Jesus desires an exclusive love from His church, a love that leads us to faithfully labor in His field and to seek meaning, purpose, life, and identity in Him and in Him alone.

Behold the Redeemer Who Gives Refuge from the Lord (vv. 10–13)

Look at Ruth in verses 10 and 13. She is overwhelmed by the grace Boaz shows her. In verse 10, "She fell on her face, bowing to the

ground and said, "Why have I found favor in your sight that you
should take notice of me, since I am a foreigner?" Even after Boaz
explains he has seen her faith in action—leaving her relatives to be
joined to God's people (v. 11)—she asks, "[Why] do I find favor in
your sight, my lord, for you have comforted me and indeed have spoken kindly to your maidservant, though I am not like one of your
maidservants." A mark of someone who is truly adopted into the
family of God is a profound and unshakable sense we do not deserve
to be there. Yet, somehow, through the amazing and gracious provision of a redeemer who welcomes the outsider and makes her a child
in God's family and qualifies her to harvest in God's field—we are!

In verse 12, Boaz prays the Lord would reward Ruth's work because
she has sought refuge/rest under His wings. However, as we keep
reading, it seems Boaz is the one providing refuge to Ruth. The
commentary of Steven Fowl is helpful here:

> Although Ruth herself may not have described her
> actions in the way Boaz does, Boaz's description
> would have been recognizable to attentive Israelites.
> Psalms 17:8; 36:7; 63:7; and 91:4 all use the image of
> shelter under God's wings as a way of describing
> both a place of safety and God's care and
> compassion. The word used to designate God's
> wing, *kanap*, is the same word that Ruth will use in
> 3:9 when she asks Boaz to cover her with the corner
> of his garment.[23]

The refuge Ruth needs from the Lord comes through a redeemer
who works in concert with the Lord's purposes. Boaz does not pray
a prayer he is unwilling to be used by God to answer. He gives Ruth
the very refuge he has prayed the Lord would give her under His
wings. Here we have a human redeemer from Bethlehem giving

---

23. Laura A. Smit and Stephen E. Fowl, *Judges and Ruth, The Brazos
Theological Commentary on the Bible*, (Grand Rapids: Brazos, 2018), 229.

Ruth the Lord's refuge. In an even greater way, Jesus not only works in concert with God's purposes, He is God made flesh. Jesus is not merely one with God in purpose but one with God in essence. Like Boaz, but in an infinitely greater way, Jesus is the redeemer who gives us rest and refuge from the Lord.[24]

Behold the Redeemer Who Welcomes Us to His Table (v. 14)

In verse 14, before she gleans, Boaz calls her close and gives her bread and vinegar and a seat at the table with his other reapers. She receives more than she can even eat—she "had some left" (v. 14). As Fowl observes, "Ruth is able to eat her fill (something that she may not have been able to do for some time)."[25] This turn of events is remarkable. Ruth arrives in Bethlehem as a widowed Moabitess, and now she is welcomed to eat with all the other harvesters at the lunch break where she enjoys unlimited bread and vinegar.[26] She started out the morning empty, and now she is full.[27]

---

24. We have already covered Ruth's repentance and faith in "turning" to the Lord in chapter 1. However, this is highlighted again in verse 11. Turning to the Lord means turning away from our former sources of life, identity, and purpose. It is a wholesale change. There would, of course, be nothing to turn to unless God made a way to redeem those who repent. That happens through the grace of God which is made available through the Son of Promise who shelters us under His wing.

25. Smit and Fowl, 230.

26. I get the image of all-you-can-eat breadsticks at the Olive Garden in my mind. The workers have been laboring all morning and break for lunch, and Ruth, the Moabitess, gets unlimited breadsticks as though she had been working with them all along (Matt 20:1–16).

27. When we arrive at the New Testament, Jesus calls Himself the Bread of Life. This is a metaphor. To live physically, we must have food/bread. However, physical bread is eventually powerless to sustain physical life. We need more than the bread that extends our physical lives for a season; we need a different sort of bread—a bread that gives us a life that even physical death cannot destroy. This bread is Jesus. He comes and offers His life as the final, once-for-all sacrifice to cleanse our conscience, put away our sin, and then be raised to represent His people in the Father's presence until He returns to raise us up to dwell with Him forever in the new heavens and

Behold the Redeemer Who Gives Us Enough to Share (vv. 15–16)

After Ruth has been satisfied with Boaz's grain during the afternoon lunch break, Boaz sends her into his bountiful harvest. He makes sure she will not go home empty-handed. He tells his servants to let her glean even among the sheaves and leave bundles of grain for her. As Holmstedt writes,

> The fact that he not only allows Ruth to collect grain by following his harvesters through the field (instead of waiting until the harvest is finished) but also has his harvesters intentionally leave bundles for her goes well beyond the requirements of gleaning as it is described in Lev 19:9; 23:22; Deut 24:19–21. Leviticus 19 and 23 indicate that the "corner of the field" is to be left for those who need to glean, while Deuteronomy 24 suggests that forgotten or missed sheaves are to be left for the gleaners. In neither case, though, is the owner or harvesters instructed to intentionally leave behind sheaves from the harvest. Yet, this is precisely what Boaz is doing for Ruth.[28]

Boaz gives Ruth far more than the law requires, and he insists the harvesters treat her with dignity and respect—no insults or rebukes (vv. 15, 16). The redeemer is not the only one who welcomes the outsider, he insists that his workers welcome the outsider too. This

---

earth. We are saved through the sacrifice of Jesus, and to have true life, we must recognize that Jesus is our true food. Boaz spared no expense in welcoming Ruth to his table. He did not ask her to submit a resume or to pass a test. She only needs to come to him and be fed. Before Jesus goes to the cross, He institutes the Lord's Supper in the upper room with His disciples. The Lord's Supper is the ordinance given to the church where all the servants in God's field come together as one family and celebrate the life they have through Christ. Jesus is the greater Boaz. He does not merely give us bread and the crushed fruit of the vine; He fills them with the substance they otherwise lacked—Himself broken and bleeding—to save guilty sinners and put them to work in His field.

28. Holmstedt, 135.

again is a picture of the church extending to others, no matter their background, the grace of God that we ourselves have come to know through Christ.

In beholding Boaz, we see a picture of God's Promised Son and Redeemer. We see a portrait of God's coming Son who will give to those who come to Him empty more provision and purpose as harvesters in His field than they could ever hope or imagine.

Scene 3: Ruth Shares with Naomi and Returns to the Harvest | We must share with others and reap until the harvest is complete (vv. 17–23)

Until verse 17, Ruth has been mostly passive in her action. She walks to the fields in hope, but it is Boaz who notices her, feeds her, and commissions her to work in his field with all the protection she will need to do so with confidence. Ruth's work begins after she receives God's gracious provision through Boaz. Her work is to harvest in Boaz's field, and the same is true for us. When Christ draws us near to feast upon Him, He does it not only to fill us but also to nourish us for the work of harvesting.

Even though Ruth does not get started with gleaning until after the midday meal, she gleans for as long as she can, all the way "until evening" (v. 17). In only a half-day of harvesting, she ends up gleaning "about an ephah of barley" (v. 17) — 30 pounds worth. Imagine Ruth lugging that sack from Boaz's field back into the town of Bethlehem. It took work; it was hard, but it was surely full of joy. As Ferguson writes,

> Here is the young widow who emigrated with probably little more than the clothes on her back. That morning, she left the bare cupboards in the

> home of her Jewish mother-in-law. Now, only hours
> later, she staggers home with 30 pounds of grain
> over her shoulders.[29]

The bountiful supply that comes to us in Jesus also comes with a
commission to take His provision to others who are spiritually starv-
ing. Though this Kingdom-expanding work comes with challenges,
the joy that the formerly hungry find when welcomed as laborers in
Jesus's field is more than enough to sustain them in the work of harvesting by sharing Jesus with others.

In verse 18, Ruth is again "satisfied" (see v. 14), and she has plenty
left to share with Naomi. This is a picture of how God provides for
us in Christ. In the miracle of the feeding of the 5,000, Jesus multi-
plies the bread and they "all ate and were satisfied" (Mark 6:42). In
the miracle of the feeding of the 4,000, Jesus uses the disciples to dis-
tribute the bread, and the bread just keeps on coming. Seven loaves
become enough bread for 4,000 with leftovers. Ruth is showing us
that true satisfaction comes from a redeemer who is able to keep
supplying us with nourishment we can give away and lose nothing
in the process.[30] The provision Ruth finds in Boaz's field is a picture
of the unending spiritual nourishment available in Christ who came
to rescue sinners. As the chorus of the hymn "Room at the Cross"
reminds us:

> There's room at the cross for you,
> There's room at the cross for you;
> Tho' millions have come,
> There's still room for one;
> Yes, There's room at the cross for you.[31]

---

29. Ferguson, 54.

30. This, of course, is a point that even the disciples are slow to
understand (see Mark 8:14).

31. Ira F. Stanphill, "Room at the Cross," Singspiration Music, 1946. As
presented in *The Baptist Hymnal* (Nashville, TN: Convention Press, 1991),
315.

In verse 19, Naomi asks, "Where did you glean today, and where did you work?" Naomi also invokes a blessing on whoever noticed Ruth, and Ruth gets straight to the point. She answers Naomi's question not with a "where" but a "who."[32] We can almost imagine Ruth saying, "It is not where I worked that matters. You need to know the name of the one who 'took notice' of me (v. 19, recall v. 10). I worked with Boaz."

This is what it looks like when desperate sinners are fed by the all-sufficient Christ. People will ask, "What's different about you? What program did you try? What steps did you follow? Where did you go?" The answer of those who are fed by the redeemer goes something like this: "It was not a program. It was not steps in a self-improvement plan. It was not time away on vacation. It is Jesus, God's Redeemer. He is where I found the true bread that satisfies my soul."

Notice what happens as Naomi hears this news. Just as Boaz's servants did in verse 4, Naomi blesses Boaz (v. 20). The one who left behind God's people and returned to Bethlehem "bitter" (v. 1:20) is now pronouncing blessing on Boaz like one of the harvesters in his field.[33] Then Naomi proceeds to foreshadow the rest of the story as she says that, through Boaz, "the Lord...has not withdrawn his kindness to the living and the dead" (v. 20). This word "kindness" is the word *hesed* noted in chapter 1:8. Ruth's faithfulness to Naomi and later to Boaz (v. 3:10) is a reflection of the kindness she receives from the Lord who is faithful to keep His promise to all who turn to Him

---

32. Holmstedt, 140.

33. This is what happens when we receive God's grace through God's Promised Son and Redeemer. We share Him with others who need His provision, and when they receive His provision of a gracious salvation, they are changed from being bitter to those who bless. They become like His other workers.

by sending a Son who satisfies our every need. When you are filled by God's promised Son and redeemer who graciously extends the *hesed* of the Lord, your redemption has begun.[34]

Naomi exclaims of Boaz, "The man is our relative, he is one of our closest relatives" or, better translated, "the man is near to us, one of our redeemers." In chapter 3, we will examine the concept of the near redeemer more closely. For now, Fowl's summary is helpful. He writes,

> When applied to God, the term refers to God's capacity to rescue one from danger or distress. When applied to humans, the redeemer is one who can buy back land that has been sold to outsiders out of economic necessity, or buy back people sold into slavery (Lev 25:24–25, 47–55).[35]

Perhaps there is hope after all, not only for Ruth and Naomi to be abundantly satisfied with grain but to have someone perpetuate Naomi's family name, a name that was otherwise dead, and give them a standing in the land. Could this Boaz be the one to raise up a son in the place of Naomi's dead sons? That question remains unanswered for now, but things are certainly looking up!

For now, we should notice Ruth was after more than a mere meal to satisfy her immediate problem. After one day of gleaning, she had come home with enough barley to meet the needs of two widows for weeks. But, in verse 21, Ruth says that Boaz had invited her to continue to take part in the harvest alongside his servants. As Holmstedt

---

34. The kindness/mercy Ruth showed to Naomi (v. 1:8) in Moab is a kindness that came ultimately, not from Ruth, but from the Lord. Ruth's actions in chapter 1 reflect the character of the man through whom God begins to bring redemption in chapter 2. This is true of the church as well. When we are rescued through God's Man, we take on His nature. For kindness (*hesed*) is a part of his very name (Exod 34:6).

35. Smit and Fowl, 231.

writes, "Boaz is already fulfilling at least part of the redeemer's role by providing for the women on a longer-term basis."[36] Boaz's provision, like the provision of Jesus, comes to those who are enlisted as laborers in his field. Redemption is not merely for us but for others as well. Those who are redeemed by the Redeemer from Bethlehem are those who willingly and eagerly keep returning to the Redeemer's field to participate in His harvest.

Ruth, for her part, is ready to go back noting that Boaz had given her permission to remain with his servants until "they have finished all my harvest." Naomi, perhaps hoping for an opportunity for Ruth to marry Boaz, urges Ruth to stay close to Boaz's maids and not to his male servants. However, as we close chapter 2, the emphasis is on Ruth's continued work as a full partner in the work of the harvest. Ruth accepts Boaz's proposal, working in his harvest and remaining with Naomi.

This is a picture of what happens in the life of one who is redeemed by Christ. When we really taste of Christ and see that He is good, we continue to feast upon Him not by keeping Him to ourselves but in sharing Him with others. In Matthew's gospel, we read about the need for workers in God's harvest.

> Seeing the people, He [Jesus] felt compassion for them, because they were distressed and dispirited like sheep without a shepherd. Then He said to His disciples, "The harvest is plentiful, but the workers are few. Therefore beseech the Lord of the harvest to send out workers into His harvest" (Matt 9:36–38).

Now that Christ has come as the Bread of Life, sharing Him with others is how we participate in our Redeemer's harvest. If Christ has

---

36. Holmstedt, 143.

redeemed you, you have been redeemed to embody Christ's compassion for those who still need to hear of Him and trust Him. He has saved you to send you into His field, and He does not send you alone. He sends you as a part of His church, His servants, people who "stay close" (v. 21) to one another and support one another in our Redeemer's field until the harvest is done.

May God find us faithful to feast upon Christ our Redeemer. May we regard ourselves as a bunch of undeserving outsiders filled up to overflowing by God's miraculous provision for our lives in Christ, and may He find us eager to share His Promised Son and Redeemer with others, reaping in His harvest until the harvest is finished.

QUESTIONS FOR PASTORS AND TEACHERS

1. How much of the concept of kinsman-redeemer should I feature from chapter 2, and how much should be saved for chapter 3?[37]

2. How much time should I spend justifying the use of Boaz as a type of Christ?[38]

3. What New Testament texts show the church as happy harvesters in God's field?

---

37. I decided to preview the concept in this chapter but to give it a more full treatment in chapter 3 when the discussion of the nearness of Boaz's relationship to Naomi's husband comes into focus (e.g. 3:12–14).

38. I have written the introduction to this text to help us understand that neither Boaz nor Obed need to be specifically referenced in the New Testament as types of Christ, because the Old Testament itself urges us to seek God's Promised Son from the very first story in the Bible. Both of these sons of Judah are rightly understood as showing us something about God's Son. In my experience, it is often easier for people to grasp Boaz as a type of Christ by spending a little time explaining the concept and simply preaching the fruit of the approach. As the people God has entrusted to you behold Christ by beholding Boaz, the Holy Spirit will do the rest. I have also found that having a discussion group following the sermon allowed me to address specific questions, and they grew more confident in reading the Bible Christologically.

4. Will I bring out the connection between the blessing of Abraham by Melchizedek with bread and wine (Gen 14:17–19) and the blessing of Ruth by Boaz with bread and vinegar (lit. sour wine)? Here we have a picture of one of the sons of Abraham bringing blessing to someone from among the nations. Ultimately, I subordinated this in my sermon but then briefly summarized this information and its culmination in Christ our forever-great High Priest in the order of Melchizedek who cleanses us with His once-for-all sacrifice of which we are reminded in the partaking of the bread and the cup.

SMALL-GROUP DISCUSSION QUESTIONS

1. Why does Ruth need to meet someone who will show her favor?

2. How is Ruth's status as a foreigner like the status of anyone who has not been saved by Jesus?

3. How does the text show us that Ruth is changing categories— leaving behind being a foreigner to God's people and being welcomed as one of God's people?

4. How can those who are strangers to God today be welcomed into God's family?

5. When do you most feel like you are not a son or daughter in God's family? What determines your status?

6. What did God lead you to leave behind when you were welcomed into God's family?

7. How does Boaz's response to Ruth help us understand how a local church should relate to people who come from different cultures and backgrounds?

8. What risks or inconveniences are most difficult for you to accept to be used by God to extend His grace to others?

9. What happenstances have happened in your life that you now know were God graciously working in the background to bring you to faith in Christ or to lead you to follow Him more faithfully?

10. What are the similarities between the workers in Boaz's field and the local church?

11. Was it selfish of Boaz to insist on Ruth staying in his field? Why or why not?

12. Who gives refuge to Ruth, Boaz or the Lord? How does the answer help us understand the refuge that we have in Christ?

13. How does Ruth's return to the field to harvest after she has already had her fill of bread relate to the mission of the church in the world?

14. What would you say of someone who says they are a Christian who never harvests or tries to share Jesus (the Bread of Life) with others?

15. Boaz allowed Ruth to eat until she was "satisfied." Why is the satisfaction that comes through God's Son the only thing that truly satisfies the human heart?

The following figure was used as illustration when we preached through Ruth at our church. Feel free to use it or adapt it as you preach and teach through the material.

The Redeemer in Ruth 2	
IS FROM BETHLEHEM (2:4)	CLAIMS THE OUTSIDER AS HIS OWN (2:8)
NOTICES THOSE IN NEED OF BREAD (2:5)	GIVES REFUGE FROM THE LORD (2:10-13)
WELCOMES THE OUTSIDER (2:6-7)	WELCOMES THE OUTSIDER AT HIS TABLE (2:14)
GIVES ABUNDANT, GRACIOUS PROVISION (2:8-9A)	GIVES THE OUTSIDER ENOUGH TO SHARE WITH OTHERS (2:15-16)
PROTECTS THOSE WHO COME TO HIM (2.9B)	SENDS THE OUTSIDER INTO HIS HARVEST WITH THE OTHER HARVESTERS (2:21-23)

Figure 1: The Redeemer in Ruth 2.

Ruth Three
The Redeemer is a Worthy Relative

In chapter 2, Ruth goes out to glean, and God gives her what she prays for (v. 2:2)—one who takes notice of her and shows her incredible kindness (*hesed*, 2:20). Boaz does not merely allow Ruth to pick grain in his field. He offers protection. He gives her bread and vinegar before sending her out into his field to harvest. He tells her to stay only in his field and allows her to gather all the way to the end of the barley and wheat harvests. When Ruth reaps in Boaz's field, she is satisfied, and she has more than enough to share with Naomi.

By the end of chapter 2, our confidence is growing that God is using Boaz to give us a picture of the lavish redemption He ultimately bestows upon His people through the gift of Jesus, His Promised Son. God the Son left heaven to be conceived in Mary, born in Bethlehem, and given the name Jesus. He came to do what His name suggests, which is to grant salvation—in the language of Ruth, redemption. He came to pay for sins and be raised up to a forever-life through which all who trust in Him may know the satisfaction that can only come to those who know Him as the Bread of Life.

While we have strong evidence the Spirit is providing a picture of the wondrous redemption available in God's Promised Son, the picture is still incomplete. Naomi and Ruth have found bread in Bethlehem, but it remains to be seen what will happen when the harvest ends (2:23). Their redemption is underway, but will God provide a way to raise the house of Elimelech from the dead and give them a standing in the land and among the people of God? The death of a son in the line of Judah has brought Naomi and Ruth near to the people of God, but we must keep reading to see if God will raise up a son who can overcome the deadness of Naomi's family and save them both.

This question is at the heart of our understanding of the redemption God gives through His Promised Son. The provision of physical bread is a sign redemption is on the way, but it is not redemption. God's redemption brings with it a far more lasting and reliable provision than a good harvest for one season. The teachers of the prosperity gospel end their teaching in chapter 2 and miss the message of chapters 3 and 4. God's redemption does not ultimately come by a change in our material prosperity but through a change in our identity that is made possible through our marriage to a son who is qualified and willing to redeem us.

For Ruth and Naomi to be redeemed, they need Boaz more than they need Boaz's bread. For Naomi to be rescued, an animal or an angel will not do. She must have a son to carry on the family name and inheritance in the land. There must be someone related to her husband who will pay the price to redeem her land and give her, a woman too old to have a child, a son. What is needed is God's provision of a miracle son to take the place of her dead sons—a son who will redeem.

Boaz seems to be a possible solution. But the harvest seasons are end-
ing, and nothing has happened. Naomi grows impatient and devises
a plan to at least help Ruth. As a result, we get a look at the character
of Bethlehem's Redeemer.

Scene 1: The plans of an impatient mother-in-law | The faithful should wait upon the Lord (vv. 1–6)

In chapter 1, we saw Naomi's repentance in her return to Bethlehem. We also saw her confession that she was pleasant when she was
full of herself and had a full house, but when God emptied her, she
was bitter. She was starting over in Bethlehem with only the Lord.
She was exactly where we must be to know and enjoy the wonder of
being filled by the Lord. To be redeemed by the Lord, we must first
know the emptiness of self-reliance.[1]

Now, as we saw in chapter 2, Naomi has been filled. In accordance
with God's Word, Ruth went out to glean.[2] She happened upon
Boaz's field, and both Ruth and Naomi were filled because of God's
lovingkindness to them through Boaz (v. 2:18).

However, after she has been graciously filled, Naomi returns to
making plans to provide for herself. God is already proving He will
provide, but Naomi decides to try to speed things along. As chapter
3 begins, she asks two rhetorical questions which assume a positive
response. "My daughter, shall I not seek security for you... (v. 1)?
Now is not Boaz our kinsman" (v. 2)?[3]

---

1. This is the ongoing need of those who are children of the Father
through faith in His Promised Son. This fullness is supplied through the
Spirit's miraculous and ongoing application of what Jesus has accomplished
to the mind and heart of the people of God (e.g. Eph 5:18).

2. E.g. Lev 19:9–10, 23:22; Deut 24:19.

3. The word that Naomi uses, kinsman, is not the word go'el (kinsman-
redeemer or nearest relative), but in verse 9, Ruth does use go'el. Both

Naomi is not asking Ruth's opinion. She is speaking like a prosecuting attorney making opening remarks. Her rhetorical questions are designed to justify the course of action she will suggest. Naomi desires for Ruth the "security" (literally "rest") that comes through marriage. Her desires are good, but as we will see, her methods are not. She is willing to put Boaz and Ruth in a morally-compromised situation to secure Ruth's redemption and standing among God's people.[4]

In verse 2, Naomi says Boaz is "winnowing grain tonight." She is not interested in waiting for daylight. What man in his right mind would marry a widowed, childless, Moabite woman with a needy mother-in-law? So, Naomi opts for less-than-honorable tactics under the cover of the darkness. Naomi so desperately wants her will to be God's will that she fails to wait upon the Lord, and risks the redemption that God has in store for her in the process.[5]

Naomi tells Ruth "wash yourself, anoint yourself, and get dressed" (v. 3). Holmstedt argues that at a minimum, "The bathing, perfuming, and dressing...suggest Naomi intends for Ruth to present herself to Boaz as a potential bride."[6] Washing, anointing, and

women know Boaz can be a *go'el*, and Naomi has apparently communicated that to Ruth.

4. Naomi's motives, at least on the surface, are good. For Ruth to have reliable provision in the land and be grafted into the people of God, marriage is the ideal. In this way, Ruth legally becomes a part of the family without having to rely on gleaning laws to have food. However, what Naomi proposes next seems to be aimed more at a stealthy sexual encounter along the lines of Tamar and Judah (Gen 38) than a proper marriage. This suggests she may be interested in Ruth having a son with Boaz, someone she has already stated is a near relative to her husband, so there would be an heir in her family to perpetuate the family's standing among God's people.

5. One can envision many scenarios in which Naomi's plan would have backfired and left both her and Ruth without redemption.

6. Robert D. Holmstedt, *Ruth, A Handbook on the Hebrew Text*, (Waco, TX: Baylor U Press, 2010), 151.

dressing are terms used in Ezekiel 16:8–9 to describe what the Lord did for Israel in making her His bride. The Lord says through His prophet,

> "Then I passed by you and saw you, and behold, you were at the time for love; so I spread My skirt over you and covered your nakedness. I also swore to you and entered into a covenant with you so that you became Mine," declares the Lord God. "Then I bathed you with water, washed off your blood from you and anointed you with oil..." (Ezek 9:8–9).

Naomi seeks marriage for Ruth, but her methods are risky and rash. It is nighttime at the threshing floor, a common place of prostitution. In Hosea, the prophet condemns the faithlessness of Israel to her covenant with the Lord:

> Do not rejoice, O Israel, with exultation like the
>   nations!
> For you have played the harlot, forsaking your God.
> You have loved *harlots' earnings on every threshing*
>   *floor* (Hos 9:1, emphasis mine).

So, while Naomi uses the language of marriage, the setting is designed for subterfuge.[7] In God's relationship with Israel, it was the Lord who initiated the covenant and extended his lovingkindness (*hesed*). In this arrangement, Naomi knows that she and Ruth need the lovingkindness of God, but she still does not understand the Lord freely gives mercy to those who recognize their need for it and humbly request it. It does not need to be coerced or manipulated.

---

7. Laura A. Smit and Stephen E. Fowl, *Judges and Ruth, The Brazos Theological Commentary on the Bible*, (Grand Rapids: Brazos, 2018), 235.

Naomi tells Ruth to not approach Boaz until "he has finished eating and drinking" (v. 3) likely because, as Holmstedt observes "a man with a full stomach is more easily persuaded."[8] Fowl sees in Naomi's overall instructions to Ruth a sort of recapitulation of the twisted sexual history that has led them to this point. He writes:

> Naomi's plan seems similar to the plan that Tamar executes in Gen 38, securing a future for herself through Judah. This fits with the explicit connection between Ruth and Tamar that appears in 4:12. In addition, attentive readers will recall that Ruth descends from Moab, who was conceived when in the wake of the destruction of Sodom and Gomorrah, Lot's oldest daughter conceived a child after "lying" with her drunken father (Gen 19:33–35).[9]

In verse 4, Naomi proposes a plan for Ruth to "lie down" with Boaz. The Hebrew verb translated "to lie", *shkb* (שׁכב), occurs eight times in Ruth 3.[10] The word can refer to a sexual encounter as in the account of Lot and his oldest daughter or simply to sleeping. Naomi is clearly aiming at an opportunistic sexual encounter that capitalizes on Boaz being asleep. Indeed, while the Hebrew is ambiguous and debated in verse 4, it seems most likely that Naomi does not urge Ruth to uncover Boaz's feet and lie down but to lie down at Boaz's feet and uncover herself.[11] As Fowl writes, "it is clear that Ruth is being instructed to offer Boaz a sexual encounter."[12]

Ruth is supposed to find where Boaz is, lie down at his feet, uncover herself, and wait for instructions. In verse 5, Ruth's loyalty to

---

8. Holmstedt, 137.

9. Smit and Fowl, 234.

10. Smit and Fowl, 234.

11. This makes the most sense of Ruth's request for Boaz to spread his covering (literally wing, see 2:12) over her.

12. Smit and Fowl, 235.

Naomi shines; she will do all Naomi has asked. In verse 6, that is just what she does. It is helpful to note that at this point in the story both Naomi and Boaz want Ruth to enjoy the rest that only comes through the *hesed* of God. However, Naomi still needs to learn that God's redemption is pure. Because of Naomi's impatient presumptiveness in concocting this plan, she unwittingly provides the circumstances in which the supposed worthiness (recall 2:1) of this possible redeemer would be put to the test. As Ferguson writes, "Perfume, night-time, good food and wine, the warm physical closeness of an attractive woman...what man could miss the apparent message?"[13] Will Bethlehem's redeemer pass the test? Is there a redeemer who can resist immediate gratification of his desires and break the cycle of inherited baggage and sin?

Scene 2: Boaz is tested | The redeemer from Bethlehem redeems in God's way (vv. 7–15)

In verse 7, we read that Ruth came to Boaz "secretly," likely concealing her identity with the shawl (v. 15) she would soon use to carry home six measures of barley to Naomi. The secrecy adds to the suspense. Deeds done in secret are no secret to God. As Ecclesiastes 12:14 says, "For God will bring every act to judgment, everything which is hidden, whether it is good or evil." Boaz is facing a most serious test. He has a full stomach. He has worked hard at the threshing floor, and he has lain down in the pitch-black countryside outside Bethlehem. In this modern era, it is difficult to conceive of the darkness that would have characterized the rural countryside in the fields surrounding the town of Bethlehem. This is can't-see-your-hand-in-front-of-your-face darkness. Verse 8 says it is "the middle of the night." The crisis and climax of this story has come under the cover of darkness.

---

13. Sinclair B. Ferguson, *Faithful God: An Exposition of the Book of Ruth*, (Bryntirion, Bridgend CF31 4DX, Wales: Bryntirion Press, 2005), 83.

We will soon know what sort of man Boaz is. Nighttime, perfume, and a younger woman lying at his feet, and Boaz is startled awake. We should not be surprised that he is surprised! The tension is palpable. What will Boaz do? It is at this point in the story that Naomi thought that Boaz would tell Ruth (you know) "what to do" (v. 4).

Instead Boaz asks, "Who are you?" (v. 9). He does not yield to the desire for self-gratification.[14] In the pitch-black darkness of fields near Bethlehem, the selfless godliness of Boaz shines bright. He will not know this woman without knowing who she is. Faced with great temptation, Bethlehem's redeemer does not sin. In this story, Boaz is a light that darkness cannot diminish. God is at work in Boaz to paint a picture of God's Promised Son whose arrival would be gloriously announced by an angel in the fields near Bethlehem (Luke 2:8–14). He is showing us that the Promised Son will not participate in "deeds of darkness" (Eph 5:11). Boaz is showing us the Son of whom the apostle John would say, "The Light shines in the darkness, and the darkness did not comprehend it" (John 1:5).

Rather than sin in secret, Boaz asks who Ruth is. Her response in verse 9 is instructive. We read that "She answered, 'I am Ruth your maid'" (v. 9). When we come to the one who is qualified to redeem, and he asks us who we are, notice what happens. Ruth does not identify with her foreign status (see 2:10); she identifies herself as one of his own maids or female servants. Redemption does not come by way of manipulation; it comes by way of a gracious invitation. Boaz had already welcomed Ruth to be treated as a fellow worker in his field, and she has accepted that opportunity. When we

---

14. Boaz's victory over temptation in this instance reminds us of the testing of Jesus in the wilderness. After a 40-day fast, He was surely hungry, but He did not give into Satan's temptation to fill his stomach (e.g. Matt 4:1–8). He remained sinless, proving that He is the bread from heaven, perfect in our place, so that by faith in Him we could be forever filled by Him.

come to the redeemer, we are "no longer strangers and aliens, but-
...fellow citizens with the saints" (Eph 2:19).

After identifying herself, Ruth makes two requests. First, she asks
Boaz to spread his covering (literally "wing") over her. In Ruth 2:12,
Boaz had prayed Ruth would prosper under the wings of the Lord
in whom she was seeking refuge. Now Ruth is asking Boaz to be the
Lord's wings in her life. The correlation of the language used in
Ruth 2:12 and Ruth 3:9 is not accidental. The protection and re-
demption Ruth needs will indeed come from the Lord, and it will
come through the Lord's promised son and redeemer.[15]

Ruth's request suggests she understands she needs more than an encounter at the threshing floor. Lasting redemption will be possible
only if she can be brought into the family through marriage. As we
have seen, Ruth's language closely parallels that of the Lord in join-
ing himself to Israel when He says, "I spread My skirt (literally wing)
over you and covered your nakedness" (Ezek 16:8a). The parallels of
Ruth's request with the intimate language used to describe God's
relationship with Israel are not accidental. As Fowl writes,

> Ruth's actions come to stand for the Gentiles'
> longing to be joined to Israel under the corner of the
> Lord's cloak... She took the initiative to join herself
> to Naomi, Naomi's people, and Naomi's God. In
> these ways, Ruth also exhibits the great lengths to
> which Gentiles may go to be joined to Israel.[16]

---

15. This is a picture of the redemption which will ultimately come in
Jesus who is Emmanuel, God with us. God the Son left heaven to shelter us
under His wing, the wings of the Lord. For redemption to be received by
fallen people, a perfect person of proven character working in concert with
the Lord would be required. His name is Jesus, and He is God the Son, the
Lord.

16. Smit and Fowl, 239.

From the beginning, the Lord promised that in the last days people from all nations would be blessed to dwell with Him.[17] The fulfillment of this promise would come through God's Promised Son, the offspring of Abraham, Isaac, Jacob, Judah, et al. All nations are in view long before the story of Ruth is written. Israelites were never chosen as the exclusive beneficiaries of God's blessing but to be the people through whom God's Promised Son would be recognized as the only legitimate Son, Priest, and redeeming King.

The story of Ruth proves the Lord's drawing of Gentiles into His one, forever-family does not wait for the New Testament.[18] Even in this short story, Ruth has been graciously drawn to Israel's God through a son of Judah who can bring her into the family of God. Matthew includes Ruth in the genealogy of Jesus because the story of Ruth reveals God had always intended to make one new people for Himself—both Jew and Gentile—through the gift of His Promised Son. Now that Jesus has come, those who know Him are commissioned to do what Israel so often failed to do, to be a "people whose life with God and each other exudes such radiance that the world is drawn to God."[19]

Ruth does not just want to be married to Boaz for the sake of being married. She desires a relationship that will result in redemption for her and Naomi. This is why she says Boaz is "a close relative" or "a redeemer" (v. 9).

Here in chapter 3, Ruth calls Boaz "a redeemer" (v. 9) rather than "the redeemer," as he is called in chapter 4. It seems Ruth is aware of

---

17. See, for example, Gen 12:1–3 and Isa 2:1–4.

18. Jesus cites other examples. See Luke 4:24–27, and Ruth's inclusion in Matthew's genealogy of Jesus foreshadows the commission to the church to make disciples of all nations (Matt 28:18–20).

19. Smit and Fowl, 240.

others who are qualified to serve as a redeemer. We will pick this
story back up in just a moment following a discussion of redemption.

To understand how Ruth is painting a picture of the redemption
God gives through His Promised Son, it is important we understand
the concept of redemption. Lau and Goswell summarize redemption in Ruth when they write:

> Redemption of property and slaves by a kinsman-
> redeemer (*go'el*) was the most common form of
> redemption in the Old Testament. This redeemer
> was a close male relative from the same clan. The
> closer the familial relation, the greater the obligation
> to redeem on behalf of the family member in need
> (Lev 25:25). It is not restricted to immediate family
> (e.g. brother, father), since the law also includes
> uncles and cousins in the potential list of kinsman-
> redeemers (Lev 25:49). Beyond this list, any blood
> relative from his clan can redeem (Lev 25:49). In
> short, whoever can redeem a relative should do so,
> with the greater responsibility falling to the nearer
> kin.[20]

At this point, it is helpful to pause and remember that redemption
is the need of those who do not have resources to solve their own
problem. If someone could produce the resources necessary to redeem themselves or their property, there would be no need for redemption. Redemption only comes to those who have a need they
are entirely incapable of meeting.

Ruth and Naomi are incapable of redeeming themselves. They need
a near relative who is willing to pay the price of their redemption.

---

20. Peter H. W. Lau and Gregory Goswell, *Unceasing Kindness: A
Biblical Theology of Ruth*, New Studies in Biblical Theology, (Downers Grove,
IL: InterVarsity Press, 2016), 74–5.

Their inability is a picture of our inability. People are powerless to save themselves; we are "dead in our transgressions" (Eph 2:5). The good news is that the Lord delights in redeeming those who recognize their need for His redemption. Time and again in the Old Testament, the Lord powerfully intervenes and acts as a *go'el*—redeeming Israel from bondage and oppression they were powerless to overcome (e.g. Exod 15:13–16; Jer 31:11). Lau and Goswell further observe,

> Weakness is also a condition of individuals who require redemption in the Old Testament...God rescues individuals from different forms of danger, but in all instances He redeems those who cannot help themselves—the weak, the poor and the needy (e.g. Ps. 72:12–14).[21]

The story of Ruth helps us understand how a holy God would ultimately serve as a kinsman-redeemer (*go'el*) to sinful people. How can God be the near redeemer, a close relative of sinners? He would do it in the incarnation, by sending the Son, a Son called Emmanuel, God with us...and given for us.

In chapter 3, Boaz demonstrates for us the sort of worthiness that characterizes the Son who redeems. Unlike Judah, he would not need to be tricked into redeeming (Gen 38). He would gladly and willingly do so. Ruth recognizes Boaz is qualified, based on his relationship to Elimelech, to give Naomi a standing and an inheritance in the land. Ruth wants him to not only be a husband who provides for her, but a husband who redeems. Ruth is seeking a son of Judah who will both love his bride and pay whatever price is necessary to redeem. Jesus is the greater Boaz, the ultimate Son of Judah who left heaven to become a man rightly related to us, the great God-Man who came to redeem "the church of God which He purchased with

---

21. Lau and Goswell, 121.

His own blood" (Acts 20:29). The Son of God left heaven to be born as a man so that he could redeem men—so that the sinful sons and daughters of men could become saints, the sons and daughters of God.[22]

In verse 10, we learn Ruth is a young woman and Boaz an older man. She could have pursued a younger man, any younger man, whether poor, rich, or in-between. Instead, she came to Boaz because she was seeking more than a husband but a husband who could redeem her and Naomi as well. The same principle is at work when sinners run to Jesus for redemption from sin. Many other suitors are available, but there is only one husband who can save, and His name is Jesus.

The prophet Isaiah speaks of the day when the redeemed of the Lord are married to the Savior. He writes:

> It will no longer be said to you, "Forsaken,"
> Nor to your land will it any longer be said, "Desolate";
> But you will be called, "My delight is in her,"
> And your land, "Married";
> For the Lord delights in you,
> And to Him your land will be married.
> For as a young man marries a virgin,
> So your sons will marry you;
> And as the bridegroom rejoices over the bride,
> So your God will rejoice over you (Isa 62:4–5).

In the parable of the ten virgins, Jesus confirms He is the long-awaited bridegroom who alone can save. Speaking of His second

---

22. Hebrews 4–10 provides an excellent explanation of the fact that animal sacrifices were incapable of redeeming human sinners. Our redemption is possible in Jesus because He is the Lord made flesh. He is our kinsman who redeems.

coming, Jesus says, "the bridegroom came, and those who were
ready went in with him to the wedding feast; and the door was shut"
(Matt 25:10). Ruth's pursuit of Boaz is a picture of the church's
pursuit of Christ. In a world filled with false saviors, we pursue Jesus
as the only Savior who can save. We give Him our allegiance and confidently pursue Him as we await the consummation of our redemption at the "marriage supper of the Lamb" (Rev 19:9).

Ruth is in desperate need of redemption. Everything is on the line,
and notice what Boaz says next, "do not fear" (v. 11).[23] When we
come after Jesus, the ultimate redeemer from Bethlehem, He immediately puts our fears at ease. There in the middle of the night, when
Ruth has risked everything in her mother-in-law's rash plan, Boaz
says, "do not fear" (v. 11). The redeemer from Bethlehem never asks
you to compromise the integrity that characterizes those who trust
in the Lord to follow Him.

Ruth has an integrity the entire city recognizes; she is a "woman of
excellence" (v. 11). It is important to note that the word *hayil* (חיל),
which is translated "excellence," is the same word used to describe
Boaz as a man of "worth/prominence/excellence" in 2:1. While the
"man of excellence" is used relatively frequently in the Old Testament, the Hebrew phrase *esheth hayil* ("woman of excellence" or
"virtuous woman") occurs only three times (i.e., Prov 12:4, 31:10;
Ruth 3:11). In Proverbs 12:4, the *esheth hayil* ("excellent wife") is

---

23. Recall the words of the angel to the shepherds in the fields outside
of Bethlehem when Jesus is born, "Do not be afraid..." (Luke 2:10). Also
consider the words of the angel to the women who come to the tomb in
Matthew looking for Jesus who had already been raised. "The angel said to
the women, 'Do not be afraid; for I know that you are looking for Jesus who
has been crucified. He is not here, for He has risen, just as He said'" (Matt
28:5-6). Finally, as they flee the tomb, they encounter the resurrected Jesus
Himself, and we read, "Then Jesus said to them, 'Do not be afraid; go and
take word to My brethren to leave for Galilee, and there they will see
Me'"(Matt 28:10).

the "crown of her husband" associating the *esheth hayil* with the coronation of a king. In Proverbs 31, we read of the *esheth hayil* who does not need to be given strength from a mortal king because she fears the Lord. In Ruth, we have the *esheth hayil* who will (as we will see in chapter 4) marry Boaz and become a "woman of excellence" in the lineage of King David and of the Promised Messiah.[24]

The use of the phrase "woman of excellence" also reminds us of the price that must be paid to acquire her. Commenting on Proverbs 31:10, Christine Yoder observes, "This wife is not only difficult to find....She is expensive to attain. She has a 'purchase price,' and it is considerable."[25] So in Ruth, we find a Gentile turned "woman of excellence" whose redemption (as remains to be seen) is costly. Ruth stands as a shining example of the redeemed bride of Christ, the Church that was "bought with a price" (1 Cor 6:20). Paul writes of the sacrificial redemption and cleansing of the church. He writes:

> Husbands, love your wives, just as Christ also loved the church and gave Himself up for her, so that He might sanctify her, having cleansed her by the washing of water with the word, that He might present to Himself the church in all her glory, having no spot or wrinkle or any such thing; but that she would be holy and blameless (Eph 5:22–27).

It is Ruth's redemption, which this story has been revealing since she "turned" to the Lord in chapter 1, that leads to her being called a "woman of excellence." Her transformation comes through a turning or repentance that leads her to the land of the Lord where there is a son of Judah willing to redeem her. Ruth is not a "woman

---

24. I am deeply indebted to a conversation with my friend Dr. John M. Lewis for his insights here.

25. Christine Roy Yoder, "The Woman of Substance (אשת־חיל): A Socioeconomic Reading of Proverbs 31:10–31" *Journal of Biblical Literature* 122, no. 3 (Autumn 2003): 432.

of excellence" independent of her redemption. Just as Proverbs
31:10–31 is a picture of the redeemed of the Lord representing
Christ in the world, so too is Ruth a picture of someone who once
was "not a people" and now is a part of "the people of God" (1 Pet
2:10). The goal of redemption is incorporation into the people of
God, to become sons and daughters of God.[26]

Bethlehem's redeemer will do whatever is necessary to redeem, but
there is a problem here in chapter 3. There is another possible redeemer who is a closer relative (v. 12). In Leviticus 25:25, we read
that the right of redemption begins with the "nearest relative."
While Boaz is a relative who is particularly fond of Ruth and wants
to help her, there is another man who must have the opportunity to
redeem.

In Boaz, we see that the redeemer from Bethlehem knows and obeys
God's Law. There on the threshing room floor with a young, uncov-
ered woman at his feet, he is applying Leviticus 25 to his life and situation. He is like the man of Psalm 1. "His delight is in the law of
the Lord, and in His law he meditates day and night. He will be like
a tree firmly planted by streams of water, which yields its fruit in its
season" (Ps 1:2–3a). Boaz does not selfishly interpret his circumstances; he responds to his circumstances biblically and sacrificially.
Ferguson writes, "Such poise is not in us by nature. It comes from
meditation on God's Word, a life transformed by a renewed mind,
uncompromised commitment to pleasing Him, and an assurance
that His ways are best."[27] Boaz demonstrates the character of Christ.

---

26. Ruth's redemption through Boaz makes her a part of God's people
in the land. The ultimate redemption that comes through the Promised Son
of the Father results in adoption (Gal 4:5) into the family of God that brings
communion with God as Father. Lau and Goswell have an excellent
discussion of this on pp. 134–35.

27. Ferguson, 94.

After Boaz explains that he will see to it that someone redeems Ruth (v. 13), he makes a way to protect her from harm and preserve her reputation with an early departure in the morning. While there are no alternate redeemers to Jesus, the presence of another possible redeemer in Ruth serves to show us that the redemption that comes from the Redeeming Son of Bethlehem is not something he is forced to provide but something he graciously gives.

As Ruth departs, Boaz gives her a pledge of his provision as he again provides enough bread for both women (v. 15). Ferguson explains Boaz's perspective from this encounter and the sending of the six measures of barley.

> Boaz is sending a signal to Naomi...He is saying, "I understand the need, and I understand the panic. I understand why you did this. I don't approve. But my heart is open to you in grace, and this is a little message to you. Trust in the provision that God will supply."[28]

Once more the gracious provision of bread suggests that Boaz will be the redeemer.[29] However, for now, both the temptation at the threshing-room floor and the presence of another possible redeemer reveal the unimpeachable character that will characterize God's Promised Son, our Kinsman-Redeemer, the One who would be "tempted in all things as we are, yet without sin" (Heb 4:15). The

---

28. Ferguson, 99.

29. When bread is graciously provided, it is a sign of the coming reversal of the accursed state of creation brought about by the first sin. In Genesis 3:19, we read, "By the sweat of your face You will eat bread, Till you return to the ground, Because from it you were taken; For you are dust, And to dust you shall return." Ruth and Naomi are not eating by the sweat of their faces but by way of the gracious provision of a worthy son of Judah who is willing to redeem them. In Jesus, the Bread of Life broken for us, we have the pledge that the promise of life in a curse-free, new heavens and earth is on the way.

redeemer from Bethlehem redeems in a way that is consistent with God's character and God's law.

Scene 3: Waiting for the Solution | We must wait on the Lord and trust the Redeemer will act on behalf of those who come to Him (vv. 16–18)

In verse 16, Naomi does not ask Ruth, "How did it go?" but, literally, "Who are you?" It is the same question Boaz asked when he was startled awake at the threshing floor (v. 8). Naomi wants to know if she is Ruth as she has known her or Ruth as a woman betrothed to Boaz. Being married, or united, to the redeemer from Bethlehem is ultimately an issue of identity. When Ruth marries Boaz, she will forever be different. Likewise, when sinners trust in Jesus they are forever changed at the root of who they are. Redemption ultimately rises and falls on this question: are you united with the Son of Promise who is qualified to redeem?

The full rescue Naomi desires for Ruth cannot come to her unless she is married to someone who has the resources to provide for her. This is a picture of Christ and His church. Salvation is more than mere knowledge about Jesus; it is a miraculous union with Jesus who alone can give us what is required for redemption. He can give us what we need to be redeemed because He has paid the price of sin and conquered death, and He was qualified to do it. He was not just a worthy man, but a sinless man. We cannot redeem ourselves, but if we turn from our sin and trust in Jesus, the ultimate redeemer born in Bethlehem, we can be. Like Ruth, we can be redeemed and adopted into God's family.

Paul calls this miraculous reality being "in Christ." This happens when the Holy Spirit regenerates our hearts and applies the life, death, and resurrection of Jesus to our lives (see Titus 3:5). His death becomes our death, and His victorious resurrection becomes our victory—victory now as we are raised spiritually to live for the glory of Jesus and victory ultimately as those who will be raised bodily to life everlasting to dwell forever with our redeemer and feast at His table in the new heavens and earth.

As we know, Ruth's union with Boaz must wait for the final act. It is like that for the church as well. We are united with Christ by faith; we know the indwelling presence of the Holy Spirit, but we wait for the consummation of our forever-union with Christ in the new heavens and earth. In the meantime, the Redeemer from Bethlehem does not leave us empty handed (v. 17).

The lesson of Ruth 3 is clear. We do not need to devise our own plans (leaving Bethlehem, sending Ruth on a risky mission); we only need to come to the worthy redeemer from Bethlehem, and He will fill us. When we stop our restless scheming, run to Jesus in order to rest in Him, we enjoy the truth of Isaiah 40:31, "They who wait for the Lord shall renew their strength; they shall mount up with wings like eagles; they shall run and not be weary; they shall walk and not faint."

Naomi is learning, as we all must learn, that there is never a good reason to run ahead of God. Naomi is becoming pleasant, not through a trust in her own resourcefulness, but through a confident trust in what the Lord will accomplish through Boaz. We know she is learning because she now gives wise counsel to Ruth—"wait" or, more literally, "sit down" (v. 18).

Imagine for a moment Ruth's adrenaline-laced thoughts as she returns early in the morning with little sleep and under the cover of darkness. I suppose her mind was racing with questions. "Have I failed Naomi? Will she be disappointed? At least I brought home some bread."

In verses 17–18, Ruth explains what happened and Naomi understands God is God, and she is not. She says to Ruth, sit down. Stop pacing. It is okay. You can rest (recall v. 1).

They can rest because God's redeemer from Bethlehem is a worthy relative. We cannot trust in ourselves, but there is a redeemer we can trust. He notices us in our need, and He does not rest until the issue of redemption is settled (v. 18). His name is Jesus.

The promise of the gospel according to Ruth is that there is rest, security, and provision under the wing of God's redeemer from Bethlehem. We can rest when we stop our striving, planning, and scheming and come to Jesus. Jesus is the kinsman-redeemer from Bethlehem who left heaven to assume our humanity. He has done all that was necessary for the emptiness of our sin and scheming to be replaced with the fullness of life that is available in Him. Cease your striving. Sit down. Trust in Jesus, the redeemer from Bethlehem.

THE CHALLENGE FOR PASTORS AND TEACHERS IN CHAPTER 3

By chapter 3, the challenge for the preacher and teacher is summarized by this question: How will I cover the tremendous convergence of themes that emerges in these verses (e.g. redemption by marriage, redemption by a near relative, God as redeemer, a son of Judah as redeemer, the character of the redeemer and those he redeems) without 1) being overly repetitive with content from chapters 1–2 and 2) leaving enough of the story untold to complete the series in chapter 4? In this sermon, I chose to drill down on some key terms and themes, but each theme could be developed further.[30] Overall, my goal was to keep the sermon moving by focusing primarily on Boaz because Boaz is giving us a picture of the character of Jesus. However, I also spent some time on Ruth because she is showing us much about the church—her redemption and her character as one who has become a new creature with a new identity "in Christ." All of this (and more) is in Ruth 3, and a sermon-discussion small group provides a helpful format for following the many themes presented that reach their climax at the threshing floor in Ruth 3.

SMALL-GROUP DISCUSSION QUESTIONS

1. What is right about what Naomi says to Ruth at the beginning of this chapter?

2. What is wrong about what Naomi says to Ruth at the beginning of this chapter?

3. What are some ways you have seen Christians grow impatient with God and try to help Him out? Why is this unwise?

4. What are some reasons why Boaz might reject an up-front, in-the-daylight marriage proposal from Ruth?

5. What does the New Testament say about deeds done in darkness?

6. How is the scene on the threshing room floor like the temptation of Jesus in the wilderness?

7. What is the significance of Ruth using the same language that the Lord used to describe His covenant with Israel?

---

30. Once more, I must commend the book *Unceasing Kindness: A Biblical Theology of Ruth* referenced throughout this book.

8. How does Ruth's desire to marry Boaz relate to the relationship of the church and Jesus?

9. How does the need for a near relative to redeem relate to the incarnation of God the Son?

10. Does a Christian woman have to be and do everything that is found in Proverbs 31:10–31 to be a godly woman? Why not? What is this ideal portrayal of "the woman of excellence" meant to signify?

11. Why do we so often struggle to sit down and "wait" (v. 18) upon the Lord?

12. What are you facing in your life right now that we can pray about that is requiring you to trust that Jesus is enough as you wait confidently on Him?

The following figure was used as illustration when we preached through Ruth at our church. Feel free to use it or adapt it as you preach and teach through the material.

BOAZ	JESUS
No sin at the threshing floor	No sin at all (Heb 4:15)
A near relative/kinsmen redeemer	Left heaven and became a man to redeem people (Phil 2:7; Heb 2:9)
Gives the foreigner a new identity (i.e. daughter)	Turns strangers to God into God's people (Eph 2.19; 2 Cor 5:17; 1 Peter 2:10)
Pursued by Ruth	Pursued by His people (Phil 3:8-16)
Knows and keeps God's Law	Knows and fulfills God's Law (Matt 5:17-18; Rom 10:4)
Protects and provides for Ruth	Protects and provides for his Church (John 10:28; Heb 7:25)

Figure 2: Boaz Compared to Jesus.

Ruth Four
The Redeemer Willingly Pays a Price

Chapter 3 closes with Naomi expressing confidence that Boaz will prove to be a man who lives up to his name. Boaz means quickness or strength, and she believes Boaz "will not rest until he has settled [the issue of redeeming Ruth and Naomi] today" (3:18).[1] She expects strong and decisive action from Boaz. Chapter 4 will prove whether or not Boaz is the sort of redeemer we have hoped. Is he all talk until the time for costly action comes? Or is he really a worthy man who will redeem? Chapter 4, like all the previous chapters, unfolds in three scenes. In scene 1, we see Boaz with the nearer redeemer and the elders at the city gate. In scene 2, we see Boaz marrying Ruth and redeeming Naomi, and in scene 3, we see that this story of redemption leads to and has been a picture of an even greater redemption through God's Promised Son and King.

---

1. For the purposes of writing the sermon, I did not include a parallel to the decisiveness and intentionality of Jesus in His redemption of His bride, but the point of comparison could easily be made. In Mark's gospel, we see Jesus frequently rebuffing the crowds who only wanted to see a sign, but when it was time for Him to suffer and die, He was undeterred in getting to the cross to redeem us. Regardless of the opinion of His disciples or the agony He would face, He "for the joy set before Him endured the cross, despising the shame..." (Heb 12:2).

Scene 1: Boaz at the Town Gate | We must see that redemption is costly (vv. 1–8)

When chapter 4 opens, Boaz is no longer at the threshing floor. He is at the town's gate. Boaz is not a procrastinator, and the shift in setting is designed to help us internalize the swiftness of Boaz's action. As Holmstedt writes,

> This scene shifts almost jarringly from Ruth and No'omi to Boaz at the city gate, the nearer redeemer is quickly brought on stage, the city elders are gathered (as if they had all been standing around waiting for something interesting to happen!), and Boaz dictates everyone actions in an almost comical fashion (sic).[2]

To be sure, Boaz has had a most unexpected and unusual evening, but he does not allow a lack of sleep or perhaps a wave of second thoughts to keep him back from keeping his word to Ruth (3:13). He has come to the city gate ready to see to it that Ruth and Naomi are redeemed.

As the chapter opens, we see that Boaz "went up to the gate and sat down" (v. 1), and suddenly, the other possible redeemer appears. When the other possible redeemer comes into view (we never get his name), the author again uses the word "behold" (2:4). The other possible redeemer suddenly catches Boaz's eye. As Holmstedt writes, "from Boaz's viewpoint, the nearer redeemer was in the process of passing by when Boaz noticed him."[3]

---

2. Robert D. Holmstedt, *Ruth, A Handbook on the Hebrew Text*, (Waco, TX: Baylor U Press, 2010), 179..

3. Holmstedt, 181.

As soon as Boaz notices him, he commands the nameless other redeemer to "turn aside and sit down" (v. 1), and they sit together.[4] In verse 2, the elders that he convenes do the same. The brief and commanding language used to describe Boaz's activity indicates he is on an unstoppable mission to redeem. His purposeful intentionality is seen in his every word and action.

Boaz is at the town's gate, "a place where one can carry out legal and commercial transactions including those around levirate marriage (Deut 25:5–10), in the presence of witnesses."[5] However, Boaz does not initially discuss marriage. Rather, he explains Naomi is selling the portion of the field that belongs to Elimelech (v. 3).[6]

In verse 4, Boaz says he will buy the field if the nearer redeemer will not. The buyer would benefit from the annual harvests and assume responsibility for the remaining family. But Naomi is old and will not have any more children, so this seems to be a great deal for the redeemer—no living son or future heir would be around to retake the land in the year of Jubilee. This seemed like a too-good-to-be-true real estate deal, a very nice addition to his portfolio that would benefit him and his own heirs. Mr. So-and-So redeemer wants the land. Now we wonder, as Holmstedt puts it, "Boaz is supposed to get the land and the girl, but how can that happen now?"[7]

---

4. Certainly, Boaz knows the name of the nearer relative. He told Ruth about him in the dead of night on the threshing floor, and he recognizes him as he is passing by. By leaving the nearer redeemer nameless, the text keeps our focus on Boaz. While there are others who may offer to redeem, at any given point on the journey to Jesus, there is only one possible Son who does redeem. We will learn more about Boaz and, ultimately, Jesus as this no-name redeemer fades from the story.

5. Laura A. Smit and Stephen E. Fowl, *Judges and Ruth, The Brazos Theological Commentary on the Bible,* (Grand Rapids: Brazos, 2018), 246.

6. This is the first mention of Naomi's field, but a field was of little use without a husband or a son to work the field and to perpetuate the family beyond Naomi's generation.

7. Holmstedt, 181.

Then, in verse 5, Boaz throws Mr. So-and-So a curve ball.[8] Some-how, Ruth will be redeemed when Naomi's land is redeemed. Boaz insists she must be included even though Ruth does not fall under any of the legal categories for redemption because she is from Moab, and Boaz is not the brother of Ruth's deceased husband. Techni-cally, Boaz is not required to marry Ruth and include her in this act of redemption, but Boaz is a living demonstration of the lovingkind-ness of God. Ruth will be included one way or the other!

Once more, he is showing us something about Jesus as he exceeds the letter of the law to fulfill the spirit of the law and includes Ruth as a part of God's people. In verse 5, it is not clear whether Boaz is saying the unnamed redeemer must raise up an heir to Naomi by marrying Ruth or whether Boaz is saying, "that's fine, you can re-deem the land, but I'm going to take Ruth for my wife and raise up an heir to Naomi."

On either reading, the primary point remains the same. Mr. So-and-So reverses his decision because he is unwilling to "jeopardize his own inheritance" (v. 6). As Lau and Goswell explain in the follow-ing:

> Since the property would be inherited only by any son produced with Ruth: it would not be divided among the nearer kinsman's other sons. When the property was transferred to the heir who would continue Elimelech's family line, any benefit of the produce of the land would be lost.[9]

---

8. Smit and Fowl, 246. Fowl describes the unnamed redeemer as "so-and-so" based on what Boaz calls him in v. 1. Lau and Goswell also refer to the unnamed potential redeemer as "Mr. So-and-So."

9. Peter H. W. Lau and Gregory Goswell, *Unceasing Kindness: A Biblical Theology of Ruth*, New Studies in Biblical Theology, (Downers Grove, IL: InterVarsity Press, 2016), 123.

The nearer redeemer only wants to pay the cost of redemption if it benefits him.[10] When he sees the high price he must pay with no long-term advantage to himself, he backs out and signifies it with a sandal in accordance with their custom and the words of Deuteronomy 25:10. When describing a brother who would not marry his widowed sister-in-law to raise up a son to perpetuate the family line, Moses writes, "In Israel, his name shall be called, 'The house of him whose sandal is removed.'"

The introduction of Mr. So-and-So in the story of Ruth proves that redemption is not only about God's lovingkindness but also about a payment. In literary terms, we could say that Mr. So-and-So functions as a foil for Boaz. In a chapter that is "all about preserving names,"[11] Mr. So-and-So remains nameless. His unwillingness to pay the price of redemption helps us appreciate that redemption is more than mere kindness; it is kindness that comes at a great cost.

In the Old Testament, the costliness of redemption is featured prominently in the Passover. God redeems Israel from slavery by purchasing them or acquiring them as His own (Exod 15:13–16). This happens in the tenth and final plague when God delivers Israel by killing the firstborn sons of the Egyptians but passing over the firstborn sons of Israel because they put the blood of a lamb on the lintel and two doorposts of their dwellings. God took the lives of the sons of the Egyptians (Isa 43:3) and spared the firstborn sons of Israel by allowing them to substitute a lamb. A son had to die for the

---

10. As we think of the characters in Ruth as types (e.g. Boaz as a type of Jesus; Ruth as a type of the church; Orpah as someone who refused the gospel, etc.), I tend to see Mr. So-and-So redeemer as somewhat analogous to a prosperity preacher; he is (or at least should be) equipped with the information to bring a message that will lead to redemption but instead he focuses on his own enrichment while his hearers remain unredeemed.

11. Iain M. Duguid, *Esther and Ruth, Reformed Expository Commentary*, (Phillipsburg, NJ, P&R Publishing, 2005), 183.

Israelites to be delivered, and a son had to be spared for their families to persist and thrive in the Promised Land. Their sons were no more deserving than the sons of Egypt, but at the cost of the life of a lamb, God spared their sons. The Israelites were commanded to remember the Passover and to redeem their firstborn sons by paying five shekels to the priests when their son was one month old (Exod 13:13–15, Num 3:47–48).[12]

The ongoing requirement of a redemption price for the firstborn sons of Israel suggests there is a need for a firstborn son of Israel to die for full and final redemption (not merely from physical slavery but slavery to sin and death) to be accomplished. There have been clues about this from before the time of the Passover. In Genesis 3:15, God promises that a son will come to bruise the head of Satan but whose heel would be bruised in the process. In Genesis 22, Abraham takes Isaac up Mount Moriah to sacrifice him, believing God would raise him from the dead if necessary to keep His promises and deliver His people. Isaac is not sacrificed. God provides a substitute ram and a promise. One day, on the mount of the Lord, He will provide the necessary sacrifice for the redemption of His people (Gen 22:14).

True redemption will require more than the blood of lambs or the payment of shekels; it will require the death of a worthy, firstborn son of Israel. He will be a son who is willing to pay whatever price is necessary to end the curse of death and raise up to a whole new way of life all the sons and daughters He redeems. The author of Ruth highlights the price of Naomi's redemption because it is a picture of the costliness of our redemption. For we "...were not redeemed with perishable things like silver or gold from your futile way of life inher-

---

12. Lau and Goswell, 125-126.

ited from your forefathers, but with precious blood, as of a lamb unblemished and spotless, the blood of Christ" (1 Pet 1:18–19).

In Ruth, few are qualified to redeem by way of their relationship to Elimelech, and as we discover in scene two, only one is willing to pay the price to redeem. As the biblical story of God's Promised Son unfolds, some try to avoid the cost of redemption (consider Judah in Genesis 38 and Mr. So-and-So here in Ruth). The story of Ruth and Boaz demonstrates there is a redeemer who is qualified to redeem, and he will redeem without reservation and at a great personal expense. The lavish and costly kindness Boaz offers to Naomi and Ruth points to an even more costly redemption through Jesus, God's Promised Son, the One who set aside the privileges of His deity to redeem us by His death and resurrection (Phil 2:5–11).

Scene 2: Marriage and Redemption | We must see that redemption comes when a qualified redeemer willingly pays the price of redemption, unites himself with the redeemed, and gives his Son to raise the sons of men (vv. 9–16)

In verses 9–10, Boaz does what he promised to do. He pays the price Mr. So-and-So would not pay. Boaz shows that God holds nothing back from those He rescues when He redeems.

Notice verse 9. Boaz buys both what belongs to Elimelech and his sons, Chilion and Mahlon. The mention of Elimelech's sons is not an inconsequential detail. If one of his sons had survived and returned with his wife, there would have been no need for the redemption of Elimelech's property. There would have been continued hope for a son to be born to inherit the property and perpetuate his family's name in the land. Though they had wandered for a time in Moab, there would have been hope for the family to rejoin God's people upon their return. There would have been hope that future generations would live in faithful anticipation of God's coming Son of Promise.

However, that is not what happened. Elimelech died. Then, his sons died. As we read the progression of events in chapter 1, it does not seem Naomi has any interest in returning to Bethlehem until after her sons die. Only then do we read, "Then she arose with her daughters-in-law that she might return from the land of Moab" (1:6a). The death of her sons opens her heart to hear the good news that "in the land of Moab...the Lord had visited His people in giving them food" (1:6b). Naomi's redemption begins with the death of her sons. When there are no sons to provide for her physical needs, no sons to carry on the family name, she finally considers her need for the Lord's provision.

The same is true for us. To understand why it is such good news that Jesus came to die, we must understand our sin brings and even deserves death and forever-separation from God's people. Naomi is a picture of this death and separation in Moab. She seemingly had things under control until her sons died. The death of her sons awakens her to the need to turn to the Lord and be rescued by Him. For Naomi to be rescued, she not only needed a kinsman-redeemer to purchase her land but a son to take the place of her dead sons— someone like Seth, who was born and lived in the place of Abel (Gen 4:25).

The only hope for Elimelech's family is that he would have a son who could "raise up" his name (v. 10), a name that would otherwise be cut off from the land forever. For there to be redemption, there must be a resurrection. Jesus accomplishes the greater redemption, not merely perpetuating the names of those He saves but also giving them life eternal in the new heavens and earth. Jesus is the Son from Bethlehem. He is the one sent from heaven who dies the death that all the children of Adam deserve so that through His resurrection they might overcome death and become the sons and daughters of God. The death of a son leads to the search for salvation. Only the resurrection of a son can bring salvation. In Jesus, we see both death and resurrection bringing redemption, and Ruth teaches us to expect this in the coming Son of Promise.

Elimelech and Naomi need a miracle son. Boaz goes beyond the requirement of the law (he is not a brother of Mahlon, Chilion, or Elimelech), and he marries Ruth. The elders of Bethlehem view this union with great anticipation. They hope that Ruth, a barren widow, will be "like Rachel and Leah." They hope God will use her, a Moabitess no less, to be a builder of Israel. This hope and its fulfillment in the birth of Obed connect the story of Ruth and God's covenant with Abraham.

The Lord promised Abraham a son by way of his barren wife Sarah, and He miraculously enabled the conception of Isaac in their old age. Isaac and Rebekah had Esau and Jacob after Isaac prayed for the Lord to open her womb (Gen 25:21). God said His promises would be fulfilled through Jacob. Rachel and Leah, though they both dealt with barrenness at times, ultimately accounted for many of Jacob's sons. So often, when it seemed Israel would cease to exist, the Lord made a way for the birth of a miracle son leading to miraculous multiplication of the people of God. When those gathered at the center of town say, "May the Lord make the woman who is coming into your home like Rachel and Leah, both of whom built the house of Israel" (v. 11), they are saying, "Do it again Lord. Once more, act for the sake of Your people. Without You, we are nothing, but through Your provision, we are here. Though Naomi and Ruth are now childless, we have seen You work in similar situations to provide a son. Do it again Lord. Here in Bethlehem, give us a son who will be true bread for Your people."

As we know, the Lord answers their prayer. Boaz and Ruth have Obed, and Boaz becomes a father of many sons in God's family. Because Boaz is in the family tree of Jesus, the hopes of the people who prayed in Bethlehem are realized in Jesus Christ, the Son of God who "purchased for God with [His] blood men from every tribe and tongue and people and nation" (Rev 5:9b).

The elders also hope Boaz will have enduring wealth and fame in Bethlehem. This is ultimately achieved in Jesus, the Bread of Life and the King of Nations, who through His resurrection has "obtain[ed] an inheritance which is imperishable and undefiled and will not fade away, reserved in heaven..." (1 Pet 1:4). Finally, they hope the house of Boaz will be like "the house of Perez whom Tamar bore to Judah" (v. 12). This hope not only connects this story to God's promise to Abraham but also with His promise to Judah, the promise of a coming king who would forever hold the scepter and lead God's people (Gen 49:10). Despite the circumstances surrounding the union of Tamar and Judah, the elders are making the point that at a time when it seemed like a family line would become extinct, God gave an unlikely son, Perez. He would end up being the son to continue the family line of Judah that led to Boaz. While Boaz has conducted himself more righteously than Judah, the hope of the elders remains focused on the need for a son who will fulfill God's promises to God's people. The elders understood what so many who misread the Old Testament do not. The fulfillment of God's promises had always required the birth of God's Promised Son. They did not know if this son would be that Son, but they knew a son was necessary.

All of this suggests God had a remnant of people among those who remained in Bethlehem who had never ceased to seek forever-redemption through His Promised Son. The elders at the city gate are reading these events as we should read the text—with great hope and expectancy that the Lord would miraculously provide the Promised Son who delivers His people once for all.

Then we read in verse 13 that "the Lord enabled her to conceive." Although Ruth had been married 10 years, she had been unable to conceive. The conception of Obed in Ruth's womb is something the Lord enabled; it is a picture of the miraculous nature of the conception of the heaven-sent Son of God in Mary's womb approximately nine months before that first Christmas morning.

In Ruth, as at Christmas, it is the Lord who makes the gift of a Redeeming Son possible. God gives a son from Ruth's previously barren womb to redeem Naomi. This son is named Obed or "servant." He serves by redeeming. He is called Naomi's "restorer of life" (v. 14), and he raises up the name of Elimelech. What had been lost in self-reliance and self-sufficiency has been given to Naomi (and even Elimelech, Mahlon, and Chilion) in a miracle son. Jesus is the greater Obed, the Son who came to serve us by suffering for our sins and to raise us up from the death our sins deserve.

We do not have to wait for the New Testament to understand redemption requires the resurrection of the sons of men through God's gift of a miracle son. That message is signaled in Ruth and fulfilled in Bethlehem with the conception and birth of Jesus. Jesus is the long-awaited and long-promised Son of God, a worthy Savior unstained by Adam's sin and qualified to rescue all the sons and daughters of Adam who trust in Him. Jesus has come in the fulfillment of the promise of Ruth's depiction of Bethlehem's Redeemer. He has come to redeem, save, and rescue. He has come to pay the price for what was ours, sin and death; He has come to give us what is His, the righteousness of God and everlasting life.

When we stand back and consider the message of verses 9–16, we are compelled to worship our redeeming God. Ruth gives such an incredible picture of the gospel and God's grace in five ways.

First, we see that redemption means we have an inheritance. Boaz pays the price for Naomi's field and gives her, Ruth, and their descendants an ongoing share in the field he purchased with his own resources. When God Himself came to pay the price for us in the person of His Son, we received far more than a fertile field in Bethlehem. We become co-heirs with Christ, (Rom 8:17) with an inheritance on reserve in heaven (1 Pet 1:4). We will inherit not just land in Canaan but the whole earth (Matt 5:5, Rom 4:13). As Ferguson puts it, "It is God's declared purpose, sealed at the expense of his Son's death, to bless you."[13] As Paul says in Romans 8:32, "He who did not spare His own Son, but delivered Him over for us all, how will He not also with Him freely give us all things?" While we are strangers and aliens in this world, the world that is promised to those who trust in the Son will not fail to come (Heb 10:37).

Second, we see that redemption brings restoration. Ruth leaves a home and a family, and God gives her a home and a family. Naomi loses her sons, and God gives her a son. Naomi returns to Bethlehem empty, but God fills her stomach and her house. Whatever your sin has taken from you—your job, your family, your meaning, your mission, your purpose, your life—restoration comes through the redemption that is available only through God's miracle Son, the Lord

---

13. Sinclair B. Ferguson, *Faithful God: An Exposition of the Book of Ruth*, (Bryntirion, Bridgend CF31 4DX, Wales: Bryntirion Press, 2005), 120.

Jesus Christ. If you are like Naomi, left for dead and separated from God's people, turn to Jesus who will forgive your sin and give you a whole new life.

Third, we see that redemption means intimacy with God as a part of His multiethnic family. In this one story, the redeemer is presented as a husband, a father, and a son. Boaz is a redeemer because he marries Ruth and fathers a son. Obed is a redeemer because he is the son who comes from a father who is qualified to raise the name of Elimelech from the dead.

These relational images are also used to describe the redemption we have through Jesus, the Promised Son of God. Like Obed, Jesus is the Son sent from the Father. Like Boaz, Jesus is a husband to His bride, the Church (e.g. Matt 25:1–13). He unites Himself not only with Israelites but also with a woman from Moab. This is a foreshadowing of the multiethnic bride of Christ. When we stop trying to fix the deadness of our lives and give ourselves to Jesus, we become united with Christ the Son so that His Father becomes our Father. Indeed, Jesus has taught us to pray to God as our Heavenly Father, and Paul reminds us in Galatians 4:6–7 that "Because we are sons, God has sent forth the Spirit of His Son into our hearts, crying, "Abba! Father!" Therefore you are no longer a slave, but a son; and if a son, then an heir through God." When sinners turn from their sin and seek redemption from God's promised Son, they become a part of the family of God—a God who redeems as husband, father, and son.

Fourth, we see that redemption is about the fame of the Son. In Ruth 4:14, the women say to Naomi, "may his name become famous in Israel. The hope is not merely for a son but a famous son. In verse 11, a literal reading of the Hebrew text proves compelling. The end of the verse reads in this way: "make sons of character in

Ephratha, and proclaim a name in Bethlehem" (v. 11). The hope of
the elders is for many sons of character but the proclamation of only
one name. This story prophetically anticipates the birth of Jesus in
Bethlehem, the one who came to live and to die the cruel death on
Calvary's cross and be raised and given the name which is above every other name (Phil 2:5–11). Jesus is the famous Son for which the
elders prayed. He is the redeemer who makes sons and daughters of
character. As we read in Acts 4:12, "...there is salvation in no one
else; for there is no other name under heaven that has been given
among men by which we must be saved." Turn from your sin, trust
in the miracle Son from Bethlehem, and watch Jesus change you.
Watch him make you like those elders in Bethlehem, eager to proclaim the fame of God's Son.

The goal of God's redemption is not only our redemption; it is also
the glory of His Son (John 16:14). He redeems us, so that we will
worship His Son. And when you have truly been redeemed, worship
is the only reasonable response. As B.B. Warfield wrote,

> There is no one of the titles of Christ which is more
> precious to Christian hearts than "Redeemer"...It
> gives expression not merely to our sense that we
> have received salvation from Him, but also to our
> appreciation of what it cost Him to procure this
> salvation for us...Whenever we pronounce it, the
> cross is placarded before our eyes and our hearts
> filled with loving remembrance not only that Christ
> has given us salvation, but that He paid a mighty
> price for it.[14]

Christ the redeemer willingly paid the price for us. "Let the words of
my mouth and the meditation of my heart; be acceptable in Your
sight, O Lord, my rock and my Redeemer" (Ps 19:14).

---

14. B. B. Warfield, *The Person and Work of Christ,* (Philadelphia:
Presbyterian and Reformed, 1980), 325.

Fifth, and finally, we see that redemption comes from a son who restores our life by raising up that which was otherwise dead. We have already seen the need for a son to be born to "raise up the name of the deceased on his inheritance" (v. 10). For the fullness of redemption to come in Ruth, there must be a resurrection of the family name through the birth of a miracle son. Obed is that son. He serves that purpose, but this story of redemption points us to more than the continuation of a family name. It also shows us that the son who comes to raise up the dead is also the son who restores those who are living dead lives. At the beginning of this story, Naomi left the Lord. After a decade or more in Moab, she returned bitter, but the miracle son born in Bethlehem became to her "a restorer of life and a sustainer of your old age" (v. 17). Ruth was better to her than seven sons because God worked through Ruth to give a son who could raise her family name from the dead and bring her a vitality of life even in her old age. One day, all of these things would come together in God's ultimate Son of Promise. Jesus, born in Bethlehem, came to die and be raised so that our dead and bitter lives might be restored right now and forevermore.

We know to look beyond Boaz or Obed to a Son not yet born because that is how the story ends—with a genealogy referencing sons yet to be born.

Scene 3: The Coming King | God saves His people by sending His King, and He uses us in the process (vv. 18–22)

Ruth begins with a reminder that this story occurred during the time of the judges, a time when there was no King in Israel. It ends with King David's royal genealogy. Eventually, King David would emerge from this story.[15] There would be times in David's own life and in the lives of those who followed him where it would seem God's promises had failed. Yet, here stands the story of Ruth, a story of God's unfailing kindness given through a worthy kinsman-redeemer, a story of a son of Judah and a woman from Moab. God's redemptive work through Boaz and Obed served as a reminder that God would surely keep His promise and send a forever Son and King to redeem His people.

The emergence of King David from this story of redemption is a key indication that God will answer the prayers of His people in verses 11–15. However, He is not the ultimate answer to their prayers. To be sure, Ruth becomes like Rachel and Leah, a mother God uses to give birth to a son who builds up God's people. She and Boaz have a house like Perez, a house that once was dead, but then produces a son leading to a king who leads God's people. Ruth, both a Gentile widow and barren, becomes the great grandmother of King David; she has a son with a great name. Nevertheless, David still dies, and his reign ends with his death. The forever King from Judah would come, but He is not David.

David conquers many enemies of God's people. He is a shepherd keeping his flocks near Bethlehem. He is anointed to serve as king of God's people. But David still dies just like Boaz and Obed, which means we must keep seeking the Son of Promise. David adds to our understanding of the full, final, and forever Son of Promise, but he is not the Son. Like David, this Son would be a King, and he would conquer the enemies of God's people.

---

15. This is why Ruth is placed between Judges and 1 Samuel. Ruth provides the connection from Israel before a human king and the emergence of King David.

This Son of Promise is Jesus, who is from Bethlehem like Boaz, Obed, and David. Jesus became a man to be a near-enough relative to die for our sins. Jesus is the worthy man who did not sin though faced with great temptation. Jesus is the redeemer who paid the high price of His life for our redemption. Jesus is the husband who marries those who were formerly His enemies and makes them His own as the Church. Jesus is the servant (like Obed) who does what is required to give otherwise dead people a share in His resurrection. As the Bread of Life, He satisfies the empty who come to Him, and He can do it all because He is the King who conquered death and will never die again.

Jesus is Bethlehem's Redeemer, and God is still calling people to turn to Him, to be forever filled by Him, and to become a part of His story. When we become a part of the story of the Son, we find hope. As Ferguson observes, Ruth teaches us that God works "on the small scale of our apparently insignificant lives...[while] also working out a larger master plan for the world."[16] That is true hope! In difficulty, trial, adversity, and hardship, if we know Jesus, we know God is at work in our lives to bring His Son to still more people who need His redemption.

When our lives are purchased by Jesus, our purpose is to proclaim the fame of Jesus. We have a message the world must hear. No matter how far you have run, no matter how empty you may be, there is a Redeemer from Bethlehem who forgives and fills those who turn to Him. He is a worthy man who gave His life, and He will love you, fill you, deliver you, and lead you like no other.

---

16. Ferguson, 109-110. Incidentally, Ferguson's discussion of divine providence on pp. 12-13, 49-51, 106, and 108-110 is incredibly insightful and helpful material.

Do not let your circumstances, whatever famine there may be in
your life, drive you from a God who has already proven His faithfulness by sending His Son. Do not let the challenges you face be the
ruler with which you measure God's faithfulness. Measure God's
faithfulness by the full pardon for sin that is available through Jesus,
the Promised Son of God, the Redeemer from Bethlehem.

One day, Jesus will return and vanquish the remaining enemies of
God and His people. He will set this world aright. Until He comes,
Jesus is at work in the world winning the nations through people
who trust that God keeps His promises even through the greatest of
trials. He is winning the nations by including them in His family—
people like Naomi and Ruth—people like you and me.

When God redeems us, He does it for a purpose far greater than our
own salvation (as great as that is!). He does it so we would point others to the famous Son of Promise from Bethlehem, the worthy Son
who alone can redeem. If you are in God's family; if God has taken
you out of the land of His enemies (i.e. Moab) and made you a child
of God; if God has filled your barren life with the indwelling presence of the Spirit of His Son; if these things are true in your life, God
wants to use you as He used Naomi and Ruth. He wants to use you
to bring Jesus to the world.

The promised Redeemer from Bethlehem has come. He is the child
of Joseph and Mary in the line of David, Jesse, and Obed, the son of
Ruth and Boaz. He is the promised Son of God sent to redeem. May
God find us faithful to share Him with others so they too may be
forgiven and filled with Jesus Christ our Lord, the true Bread of
Life.

QUESTIONS FOR PASTORS AND TEACHERS

1. To what extent should we consider Naomi's dead sons a type of Christ? Their names suggest they are more a type of Adam, subject to weakness and sickness and subject to death. However, they are nevertheless sons of Judah. Without their deaths, Naomi would have not likely returned to Bethlehem. To be sure, God would have still sent His Son through someone, but we would have missed this story that so beautifully prophesies the advent of Jesus in Bethlehem in this narrative form. Jesus, though He conquered death, did allow Himself to die and to bear our sin. God uses the deaths of Naomi's sons to get her attention, and He can surely use the death of His Son, the last Adam, to get our attention as well. Though He is God, He became poor so that by His poverty we might become rich in Him (2 Cor 8:9).

2. As this story unfolds, we are introduced to Naomi, then Ruth, and finally Boaz. Before the genealogy is introduced, the characters move out of the story in reverse order: first Boaz, then Ruth, and then Naomi. What is God trying to show us about Naomi through this sequencing?

SMALL-GROUP DISCUSSION QUESTIONS

1. Why does Mr. So-and-So pass up the opportunity to purchase Elimelech's land?

2. How does Mr. So-and-So help us appreciate Boaz?

3. How does this story suggest that resurrection will be included in the redemption that comes through God's Promised Son?

4. The inclusion of Ruth in God's family comes by way of a costly marriage. How does Ephesians 5:25–33 speak of the relationship of Jesus and the church?

5. How can we cultivate intimacy with Jesus our redeeming husband?

6. What hinders the church from enjoying an intimate connection with Jesus?

7. How does Ruth portray pictures of the Gospel?

8. Do you think Naomi would still wish to be called bitter (Mara) by the end of the story? Why or why not?

9. How can we have God as our Father?

10. What is the primary reason the Father redeems people through the gift of His Promised Son?

11. How can we, like Ruth, be among those who have a part in bringing the Son of Promise to the world?

12. How has the Holy Spirit used the opportunity to see Jesus in the book of Ruth in your life?

The following figure was used as illustration when we preached through Ruth at our church. Feel free to use it or adapt it as you preach and teach through the material.

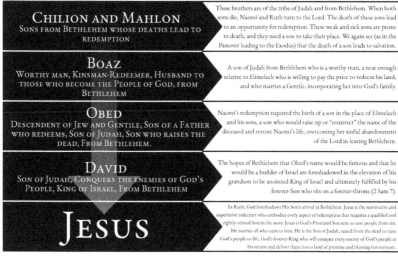

Figure 3: The Progression to Jesus.

Works Cited

Behr, John. "Scripture, the Gospel, and Orthodoxy," *St. Vladimir's Theological Quarterly* 43, no. 3 (1999).

Duguid, Iain M. *Esther and Ruth. Reformed Expository Commentary* (Phillipsburg, NJ, P&R Publishing, 2005).

Evans, Mary J. *Judges and Ruth. The Tyndale Old Testament Commentaries* (Downers Grove, IL: Inter-Varsity Press, 2017).

Ferguson, Sinclair B. *Faithful God: An Exposition of the Book of Ruth* (Bryntirion, Bridgend CF31 4DX, Wales: Bryntirion Press, 2005).

Hamilton Jr., James M. *God's Glory in Salvation through Judgment: A Biblical Theology* (Wheaton, IL: Crossway, 2010).

Holmstedt, Robert D. *Ruth, A Handbook on the Hebrew Text* (Waco, TX: Baylor U Press, 2010).

Köstenberger, Andreas J., L. Scott Kellum, and Charles L. Quarles, *The Lion and the Lamb* (Nashville: B&H Publishing, 2012).

Lau, Peter H. W. and Gregory Goswell, *Unceasing Kindness: A Biblical Theology of Ruth, New Studies in Biblical Theology* (Downers Grove, IL: InterVarsity Press, 2016).

Luther, Martin. "Preface to the Wittenberg Edition of Luther's German Writings" in *Martin Luther's Basic Theological Writings* 2nd ed., edited by Timothy Lull (Minneapolis, Fortress Press, 2005).

Quarles, Charles. "How to Read Matthew Theologically," *Credo Magazine* (December 30, 2019). Accessed from https://credomag.com/2019/12/how-to-read-matthew-theologically/.

Sailhamer, John H. *The Books of the Bible* (Grand Rapids: Zondervan, 1998).

Smit, Laura A. and Stephen E. Fowl, *Judges and Ruth, The Brazos Theological Commentary on the Bible* (Grand Rapids: Brazos, 2018).

Spurgeon, C. H. *Around the Wicket Gate* (New York: American Tract Society, 1890).

Stanphill, Ira F. "Room at the Cross" (Singspiration Music, 1946). As presented in *The Baptist Hymnal* (Nashville, TN: Convention Press, 1991).

Swindoll, Charles R. *Great Days with the Great Lives* (Nashville: W Publishing Group, 2005).

Warfield, B. B., *The Person and Work of Christ* (Philadelphia: Presbyterian and Reformed, 1980).

Yoder, Christine Roy "The Woman of Substance (אשת־חיל): A Socioeconomic Reading of Proverbs 31:10–31" *Journal of Biblical Literature* 122, no. 3 (Autumn 2003).

Scripture Index

Leviticus

Numbers

Deuteronomy

Judges

1 Samuel

Psalms

Proverbs

Ecclesiastes

Isaiah

2 Corinthians

Galatians

Ephesians

Philippians

Colossians

2 Timothy

Acknowledgements

In this book, you encounter Boaz, a man of high character, who makes the right things happen in the right way and for the right reasons. This book would not exist without some people of character who have been like a Boaz in my life. I especially want to thank my parents. My mom, Hazel, has been an excellent proofreader and a quiet and unwavering source of unconditional love and support. My dad, Dr. J. Michael Palmer, is my biggest cheerleader in life. My parents raised me to look to Jesus in all things. As we see clearly in the Book of Ruth, looking to Jesus is not just a good principle for life; it is likewise a wonderful principle for understanding the Bible.

I am also indebted to Blair Robinson, Kenneth Jones, and Robby Scholes. Blair, thank you for our many conversations about the nature of the local church and the need to align our assumptions and practices with what God has revealed in His Word. Your kindness in allowing me the privilege of discipling you helped give me confidence to lead others. Kenny and Robby, thank you for patiently enduring my endless musings about Biblical interpretation, apologetics, politics, and a host of other topics as we worked together to support Southeastern Baptist Theological Seminary. You three men are some of the greatest friends a man could have, and I thank God for you.

I am also thankful for Southeastern Seminary. It was there that I met men like Dr. Steve McKinion, Dr. Scott Kellum, Dr. Kenneth Keathley, Dr. Chip McDaniel and so many more who invested in me. It was Steve McKinion's class that helped me put together all the various pieces of the seminary toolbox in a way that points to Jesus and life in Him. Dr. Kellum is the greatest combination of humility and intellect I have ever met. I am still functional in Biblical Greek because of his excellent teaching. Dr. Keathley gave me his confidence and allowed me to teach theology under his supervision, and I learned so much through that process. Dr. McDaniel took a weary and wounded soul and became a true friend in the gospel. Southeastern was a gift of God in my life in so many ways. I thank God for the Great Commission Seminary that helped me seek the glory of Christ and the good of the nations.

Finally, I am deeply grateful for the local church. Wherever God has taken me, He has used people within my local family of faith to encourage me to keep striving for the glory of Christ. I think of men like Anthony Rice, Tom Martin, and Jim Delong who would pray with me for hours on Tuesday nights. I also think of friends like Steve who made it possible for me attend seminary. I think of men like Dr. Archie Bost who took me under his wing at Providence Baptist in Raleigh, NC and allowed me to co-teach the Book of Jeremiah with him. I think of the amazing Sunday School class I was blessed to lead at Wake Cross Roads in Raleigh, NC as well as the wise mentorship of the late Dr. Bill Bowyer. As the pastor at North Roanoke, I was blessed to preach through the Book of Ruth and receive deep encouragement from our church family. Without their enthusiastic response and encouragement, this work would not exist.

For all of these (and certainly more who are not listed), I say as Paul said of the church at Philippi, "I thank my God in all my remembrance of you, always offering prayer with joy in my every prayer for you all, in view of your participation in the gospel from the first day until now" (Phil 1:3–4).

Also Available from
College&Clayton Press

In *Bethlehem's Redeemer: Seeing Jesus* in Ruth, Daniel J. Palmer creates a Bible study for small groups or individual study that emphasizes the Messianic and salvific content contained in Ruth. This Learner's Workbook and Journal facilitates exploring even deeper with guided questions for individual study or for group discussions.

In this six-week devotional for men, Field Thigpen draws upon his ministry experience counseling and mentoring others to speak to the heart of men's uncertainties about identity, leading, and serving others. This book is not simply for young Christians seeking to mature in their faith. Thigpen writes for people who have lived, suffered, and lost. *Walk Like A Man* pushes the reader to continue maturing spiritually despite setbacks. Thigpen speaks to people in broken circumstances and points them towards God's desire to restore peace in the midst of trials.

In this updated edition of *Why Psalm 23 Is Not About You: Reading Psalm 23 in Its Context*, Dr. Robert L. Cole reveals linguistic and thematic patterns in the Psalter that demonstrates a continuity of meaning from Psalm 1 through Psalm 24. Particular attention is given to the meaning of Psalm 23 and it's surrounding Psalms. Fans of canonical studies and lovers of the Psalter will enjoy this quick, but thought provoking read.

College&Clayton
Press

ATHENS, GEORGIA

We are a publishing company dedicated to producing quality works in Christian history, theology, and biblical studies. Our goal is to help foster the love of God with the mind. We hope that such an endeavor will also lead to the love of neighbor. Our conviction is that the fruits of solid research and interpretation are more open, thoughtful, and generous individuals. Please visit our website for our upcoming titles and other articles explaining more about who we are.

COLLEGEANDCLAYTON.COM

HISTORY // THEOLOGY // BIBLE STUDY

Made in the USA
Las Vegas, NV
06 August 2022